The New Kings' Tales

By Phillip and Robert King

B.T. Batsford • London

First published in 2002

© Phillip and Robert King

ISBN 0 7134 8674 0

A CIP catelogue record for this book is available from the British Library.

Typeset by KEATS, Harrow on the Hill

Printed by Creative Print & Design, Ebbw Vale, Wales
for the publishers,
B.T. Batsford, 64 Brewery Road
London N7 9NT

A member of the Chrysalis Group plc

CONTENTS

Authors' Foreword

Having parodied a famous author, two great scriptwriters, and several fine actors, we feel that a few words of appreciation are appropriate.

Dame Agatha Christie is known throughout the world as the Queen of Crime, and she certainly made more money from murder than any woman since Lucrezia Borgia. Although she is best remembered for her *Whodunnits*, Dame Agatha wrote several thrillers best described as *Willhegetawaywithits*. *The Fatal Five* is a tribute to *The Big Four*, first published by William Collins.

Killing Defence, is a courtroom drama and an awful warning to overbearing bridge partners. It has nothing to do with work of the late great Hugh Kelsey although variations on some of his most spectacular hands are used in an attempt to fix the *Cornflakes* bridge match.

Cornflakes is a pastiche of the BBC comedy *Porridge*, a tribute to which appears on page 51.

The Time Machine is not a parody of any author or style, although any author who writes about time travel owes a debt to H.G. Wells.

The Time Machine

If you are a rather good bridge player and fancy the idea of becoming the best in the world overnight, I can tell you how to do it. It won't take years of study, practice and humiliating defeats while you measure yourself against the champions, but you may find yourself doing some rather eccentric things, like arguing with a pompous oak tree in Epping Forest.

Since, at the time of writing I am arguably the world's best bridge player, let me explain what I mean by 'rather good'. Before my elevation I had won a few tournaments, reached the semi-finals of the Gold Cup, and competed in the English Trials with some distinction.

Now I'm sure at this point you can't wait to hear about my tournament victories, but first I must explain why I was arguing with that self-important oak tree and why I eventually replanted it in my spare bedroom.

One fine summer evening, I was driving along one of those B roads which skirt Epping Forest, when I suddenly noticed a car speeding towards me – on the wrong side of the road. As I braked frantically, the madman swerved, missed my bonnet by a coat of paint, skidded off the road and crashed into a tree. When I reached the wreck, the driver was sandwiched tightly between the back of his seat and the steering wheel. He was swearing fluently.

"Are you alright?" I asked.

"Do you usually ask such stupid questions?"

"Do you usually drive on the wrong side of the road?" I countered.

"No. I forgot I was in England."

"You must travel a great deal."

"You could say that." He managed a smile, which for someone in his position was a minor act of heroism.

"You're lucky to be alive," I pointed out.

"My time hadn't come," he responded cryptically.

During this fatuous conversation, I was making a futile attempt to adjust his driving seat.

"I'm afraid it's jammed tight," I said. "I think we should call an ambulance."

"That won't be necessary. I have several superficial injuries, but no internal damage." He seemed to concentrate for a few seconds. "Pulse and blood pressure normal."

"How do you know that?"

"Believe me, I know."

"But you must be in pain."

"No, I've done something about that." He struggled to raise his right arm, which hung limply against his knee. "Look, it's obvious that I need help, but I can't afford to get mixed up with your police or your hospitals, so I suppose I'll have to trust you. Do you see my wristwatch?"

"Yes, but …"

"Please, there's no time to argue. Take it off my wrist and put it on yours."

I shouldn't have listened to him, but even while jammed helplessly against the steering wheel, the man exuded authority. He was in his middle thirties, athletically built and darkly handsome. His voice was vibrant, his manner commanding. I obediently took off his watch and slipped it on my own wrist.

"Now what?" I asked.

"In a minute I shall ask you to press your index finger against the centre of the dial and send an SOS signal. Three short, three long, three short."

"I know. I used to be a boy scout."

"Then be prepared. When you've completed the signal, a tree will materialise in front of you."

To humour him, I dutifully executed the most famous of Morse signals and found myself staring at a rather large oak tree which had appeared from nowhere.

"Bloody hell!" I gasped, maintaining the high standard of eloquence I had set.

"It's a time machine," my new friend informed me. "Equipped with a Mark Four camouflage mechanism which enables it to blend into the local flora."

I imagine that at this point most sensible people would have galloped back to their car, phoned for an ambulance and beaten a hasty retreat from the terrors of temporal paradox. But, as a lifelong fan of *Star Trek*, *Doctor Who* and *Quantum Leap*, I was far from sensible; I was hooked.

"What do you want me to do?" I asked.

"Step into the machine and tell it to go back to base."

"Will it obey?"

"It's programmed to obey whoever is wearing the watch. When you reach base you must tell them what happened. They'll know what to do."

"Are you sure you'll be alright?"

"Of course. You may be gone for an hour or so, but as far as I'm concerned the machine will reappear in a matter of seconds."

To a trekkie that sounded reasonable.

"How do I get into the tree?" I enquired.

"By saying 'Open Sesame'."

"You're kidding."

"I wish I was. I groan every time I say it."

I uttered the password, groaned for good measure, and gaped, as a section of the bark dematerialised to reveal an impossibly spacious control room. As any child aged from thirty to seventy will have guessed, I was looking at an authentic tardis.

"Pop inside," the incapacitated time lord instructed me. "Then order it back to base. See you a few seconds later."

By now my brain had returned to its customary level of semi-efficiency. I stepped into the tree, sat at the controls and said, in the most imposing voice I could summon, "Shut Sesame!"

A moment later I was utterly alone, the captain of my soul, in sole command of a time machine.

"Can you take me to any time and place I choose?" I asked it.

"Obviously not," a metallic voice replied.

"Why obviously?"

"Because time and space are infinite, and my capacity is finite," the voice sneered.

"Then how about a trip to the 1930's?"

"No problem. My database includes an extensive knowledge of that period."

"Good. But first I'd like to pop across to my house in Ilford. I live quite near a park, so ..."

"All I need is the address," the voice interrupted. "I will select the landing place."

"But it's my house," I objected lamely.

"Is this your first experience of time travel?" it asked.

"As a matter of fact, it is."

"I thought so. And you're a twentieth century primitive, aren't you?"

"It's not a description I would have chosen," I replied defensively.

"It's an accurate one."

"Why are you so rude?" I asked.

"I imagine it amused my programmer to make me so," drawled the voice.

"Is he the one who designed you to respond to 'Open Sesame?'"

"Probably. Childishness and rudeness tend to go together. But the point is that you have as much chance of understanding the principles of time travel as a Stone Age village idiot would have of comprehending quantum physics. So why not give me your Ilford address and leave the rest to me?"

Now in case you believe I am the sort of monster who would leave a fellow human being crushed like a pretzel in a contorted driving seat, I assure you that I fully intended to reappear with help from the future in what he would regard as a few seconds time.

But before doing so I was determined to have a bit of fun at the future's expense.

2

If you are planning a trip to the Summer of 1932, it is surprising how little you need to take with you to ensure that your visit will be a roaring success. A few clothes that won't look too outré in the reign of George V. Some currency of the period in reasonably good condition. And a few publications recording the results of every horse race, dog race, prize fight and other contest which offered opportunities to get rich at the bookies' expense.

For the first two nights I slept in the time machine, which had resumed its arboreal form in a wood near Epsom racecourse. A week later I moved into an expensive flat in Piccadilly and, dressed in the best ready-made clothes that money could buy, I was all set to take on the world of fashion in general and fashionable bridge in particular.

This was one of my early bridge achievements. It took place in a pleasant club which overlooked Hyde Park, and boasted a few members who could appreciate good card play.

Love All. Dealer South.

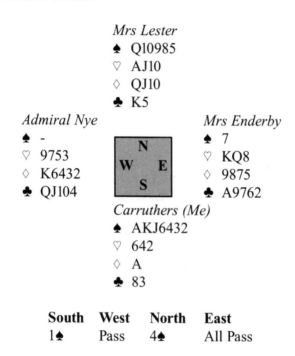

Mrs Lester
- ♠ Q10985
- ♡ AJ10
- ◇ QJ10
- ♣ K5

Admiral Nye
- ♠ -
- ♡ 9753
- ◇ K6432
- ♣ QJ104

Mrs Enderby
- ♠ 7
- ♡ KQ8
- ◇ 9875
- ♣ A9762

Carruthers (Me)
- ♠ AKJ6432
- ♡ 642
- ◇ A
- ♣ 83

South	West	North	East
1♠	Pass	4♠	All Pass

Yes, I agree that the name Carruthers is a cliché for a pre-war man-about-town, but a few weeks of employing phrases like 'Open Sesame' and 'Shut Sesame' was habit forming.

I also concede that the above auction is antedeluvian, but it worked. Now, in the 21st Century, we would have bid more constructively, explored slam possibilities, stopped at the five level and gone one off. And it so happened that making ten tricks was no picnic.

Admiral Nye led the ♣Q and as soon as dummy appeared I recognised a textbook situation, in which I might endplay East. So I played low. The Admiral, as befitted a man who had survived the Battle of Jutland, found the best defence of switching to the ♡9, which I covered with the ♡J. I won the trump exit and eliminated diamonds. Now, when Miss Enderby was thrown in with the ♣A, she had to lead away from the ♡K or give a ruff and discard. Good sound stuff, I thought, but hardly worthy of a brilliancy prize. The 20th Century primitives clearly thought otherwise.

"Well played, Mr Carruthers," gushed Mrs Enderby, a platinum blonde of uncertain years and equally uncertain card play. "Far too good for little me."

"The fellow's a wizard," said the Admiral. "It's a wonder he isn't famous. But perhaps he is. Where did you learn to play so well, Carruthers?"

"Oh, here and there, Admiral," I hedged. "New York amongst other places."

"Never been there myself."

"Interesting place," I quipped. "Something is happening all the time, most of it unsolved."

I was half afraid that the joke would be too obscure, but when they all laughed pleasantly, I remembered that by 1932 the invasion of the gangster movies was well under way.

Mrs Lester signalled the club's steward, and ordered a round of drinks. Not for the first time, it occurred to me that I could get to like the Thirties. It was the ideal age for the idle rich.

"Tell me, partner," Mrs Lester enquired thoughtfully, as the Admiral dealt the cards, "how would you have played if the defence had continued clubs?"

"A good question," I replied. "Mrs Enderby's best return at trick three would be a diamond. Now I draw trumps and discard a small heart on the ◊Q, a loser-on-loser play. Dummy's third diamond is good for another heart discard."

"So the defence only takes three tricks in the minors," said Mrs Lester thoughtfully.

"Thank goodness," said the Admiral. "I thought I might have botched things with my heart switch."

I began to pay more attention to my partner. Previously I had regarded her as a sound, careful player, but nothing out of the ordinary. Now I realised that when I had played with or against her, she had never had a chance to shine. It also dawned on me that in an unobtrusive way she was a very attractive woman, with dark, bobbed hair, warm green eyes in a pleasant oval face, shapely legs, and a figure you couldn't describe without using your hands.

After our opponents had made a partscore, and each side had sacrificed somewhat rashly, I was again the dealer:

North/South Game. Dealer North.

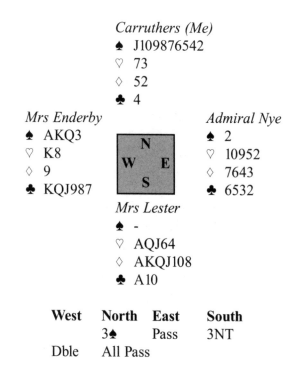

Carruthers (Me)
- ♠ J109876542
- ♡ 73
- ◇ 52
- ♣ 4

Mrs Enderby
- ♠ AKQ3
- ♡ K8
- ◇ 9
- ♣ KQJ987

Admiral Nye
- ♠ 2
- ♡ 10952
- ◇ 7643
- ♣ 6532

Mrs Lester
- ♠ -
- ♡ AQJ64
- ◇ AKQJ108
- ♣ A10

West	North	East	South
	3♠	Pass	3NT
Dble	All Pass		

Mrs Lester won the ♣K lead, reeled off her six diamond winners and exited with the ♣10. Mrs Enderby, who had kept ♠AK ♡K8 ♣QJ, gleefully cashed her four winners, but was then forced to lead away from the ♡K8 to give my partner the ninth trick.

"Oh dear," she cried. "I think I've been squeezed."

"Strip squeezed," I corrected. Daring stuff for the thirties, but the ensuing giggle suggested that I had made her day. But I made a note to find out whether the term had been invented by 1932.

"Thank you, partner," I said to Mrs Lester. "You played that with great assurance."

"She always does," said the Admiral. "Best player in the club, present company excepted of course."

"It was a faintly spectacular contract, but not difficult," she said, in her beautifully modulated voice. "The credit belongs to you, Mr Carruthers. After the double, most partners would bid Four Spades, which would not be a success on a heart lead. Thank you, for your confidence in me."

That did it. In less than ten minutes, she had transformed herself from a pleasant woman, who played a fair game of bridge, into an utterly charming, drop-dead gorgeous lady, who was destined to partner me in my bid for world renown. Mr Lester, whoever he was, should present no problem. Killing him was against my principles. But I could always dump him back in the 1890's.

3

Fortunately, Diana Lester had divorced her husband a year earlier, and he had the good grace to emigrate to Australia. She and I soon became regular bridge partners and firm friends. She was one of the quickest learners I had ever met. As a lady of leisure she had plenty of time for study and made every second count. Within a forthnight we had agreed a system way ahead of its time. Our bidding was light on conventions but strong on aggression. If our playing strength was sufficient, a lack of honour tricks never stopped us entering the auction. In short, we were nobody's favourite opponents.

A few weeks later, we won our first tournament, and fell in love. On the following evening, we had our first chaste kiss. Those who weren't alive before penicillin and the pill created the permissive society, and regard our amatory progress as unduly circumspect, should remember that in the 1930's, Fred Astaire and Ginger Rogers made eight movies in which they never kissed at all, and nobody complained. Besides, this story isn't about sex, it's about time travel and bridge, so let me tell you about the tournament we won.

It was held in a London club which no longer exists and was open to any pair who were at least friends of the friends of the organisers and could be relied upon to turn up in some decent evening clothes. Ours were extremely decent, and our bridge was not at all bad. In fact some of it was revolutionary, as you will see from this deal:

Game All. Dealer South.

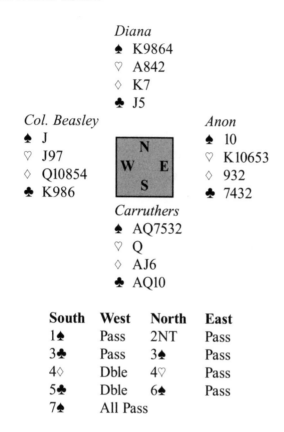

Diana
- ♠ K9864
- ♡ A842
- ◊ K7
- ♣ J5

Col. Beasley
- ♠ J
- ♡ J97
- ◊ Q10854
- ♣ K986

Anon
- ♠ 10
- ♡ K10653
- ◊ 932
- ♣ 7432

Carruthers
- ♠ AQ7532
- ♡ Q
- ◊ AJ6
- ♣ AQ10

South	West	North	East
1♠	Pass	2NT	Pass
3♣	Pass	3♠	Pass
4◊	Dble	4♡	Pass
5♣	Dble	6♠	Pass
7♠	All Pass		

I do not recall the name of Beasley's partner, but I am sure that, unlike the Colonel, he never became a famous international.

The interesting aspect of the auction was that we introduced the Jacoby raise to an unsuspecting bridge public (the Two No Trump bid showed a game forcing spade raise). Not only that, but Beasley's rash double of my cue bid enabled me to pull off a dummy reversal followed by a squeeze against West. I am aware that Jack Marx, one of the inventors of the Acol system, did the same thing fifty years before I did, but I did it twenty years before he did. So there.

Certain from the bidding that the club finesse would fail, I won the ♠J in hand, crossed to the ♡A, ruffed a heart and, crossing twice in trumps, ruffed two more.

Since the diamond finesse was equally doomed, I briefly

considered running the ◇J in the hope that Beasley would not cover. But then I decided on a more rational plan. I cashed the ♣A, a Vienna coup (no, I didn't invent it, it apparently originated in the days of whist). Next, I crossed to my ◇K and played off my two remaining trumps, discarding the ♣Q10. Beasley had to retain his ♣K, so when I laid down the ◇A, his ◇Q dropped with a satisfying thud.

"Well played, partner," Diana whispered softly.

Beasley's face was registering equal measures of awe and pique. He may have had mixed feelings about the bidding, but he was compelled, however reluctantly, to admire the play. And strangers with no pedigree were not in the habit of scoring spectacular tops against him. He couldn't quite bring himself to pay me a direct compliment, but I suppose what he said was a backhanded one.

"I don't believe I've played against you before."

"I think not, Colonel," I replied coolly. "I'm sure I would have remembered."

"So would I," he responded, with a gallant nod at Diana.

"I believe Mr Carruthers has played most of his bridge abroad," she explained.

"Really? Where exactly?" he enquired politely.

"Here and there," I hedged.

"In America?"

"Occasionally."

"New York, I suppose."

"Only at a very low level."

"You surprise me," he said pleasantly. "If you simplify your bidding system, you could go far. By the way, are you one of the Devonshire Carruthers."

"A distant connection," I improvised, wishing I'd called myself John Brown. "I'm descended from the family's black sheep."

Fortunately the director called a movement before the Colonel could delve further into my non-existent past.

We were on a roll when, at the last table, we found ourselves facing Hubert Phillips, the prolific bridge author and columnist. Although I didn't know it at the time, he was destined to be a selector of the British team to meet Ely Culbertson's all-conquering Americans.

Love All. Dealer South.

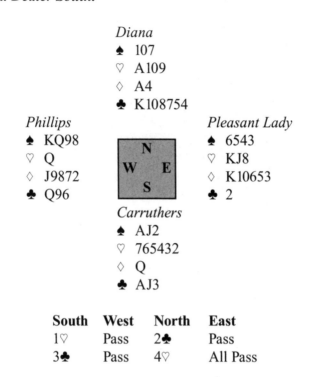

Diana
- ♠ 107
- ♡ A109
- ◊ A4
- ♣ K108754

Phillips
- ♠ KQ98
- ♡ Q
- ◊ J9872
- ♣ Q96

Pleasant Lady
- ♠ 6543
- ♡ KJ8
- ◊ K10653
- ♣ 2

Carruthers
- ♠ AJ2
- ♡ 765432
- ◊ Q
- ♣ AJ3

South	West	North	East
1♡	Pass	2♣	Pass
3♣	Pass	4♡	All Pass

When Phillips led the ♠K, my only problem was finding the ♣Q. Most declarers would draw trumps, do as much as possible to get clues to the distribution of the side suits, then take the plunge.

Being a player of the 21st century, you can probably spot the superior line. I won the spade and played a second round. Hubert (I call him Hubert because I once won his cup for mixed teams of four, and watched it gleaming on my sideboard for three months) won and switched to a diamond. I eliminated diamonds, cashed my third spade and led a heart. When the ♡Q appeared, I ducked. West was now endplayed, and if East decided to overtake, she would be in a similar position.

All lines succeed if trumps are two-two. Mine also catered for a 3-1 trump break and a singleton honour in either hand.

"A good score for you, I think," remarked Hubert sportingly. "I imagine the majority of declarers would simply play for the club queen to drop."

"With eight ever, with nine never," recited the pleasantly ample lady on my right. "But you did one of those endplays my partner is always writing about, didn't you?"

"I'm afraid so," I confessed.

"Could we have defeated you?" She asked.

"Yes, we could," said the eminent author, getting in first. "After winning the second spade I must lead the queen of hearts."

I was impressed. I wished I'd polished his cup more often.

"Not easy to find," I consoled him.

"It can't cost," he observed ruefully. "I should have seen it."

"Never mind, Mr Phillips," smiled Diana. "When the hand appears in your column you can change history by finding the winning switch."

"I shouldn't dream of it," he smiled back at her. "But may I have your partner's name?"

"Certainly. It's Colin Carruthers," she said, with some pride.

He made a note. "Should I have heard of you?" he asked.

"Not unless you read the *Police Gazette*," I replied.

"Well, I shall overlook your criminal record and give you full credit for your excellent play," he said. "But to be on the safe side, I shall say I was East."

Later that evening we celebrated our victory at a secluded West End restaurant which disproved the claim of my maternal great grandfather that in his youth you could enjoy a superb three course dinner for two, with cocktails, champagne and liqueurs, and still get change from a fiver. He had forgotten the tip.

"Colin," said Diana, as we gazed longingly into each other's eyes. "Can I tell you something?"

"Of course you can, darling," I assured her, while thinking how candlelight became her.

"Now you look like becoming a famous bridge player, don't you think we should do something about your background?"

"What's wrong with my background?"

"Well, you haven't got one, have you?"

"Haven't I?"

"You never talk about yourself. And when I ask you a question, you always answer it with a question."

"Does that annoy you?"

"It certainly ..." She broke off, and laughed. She had a rich, musical laugh. "Stop it," she chided. "I've known you for nearly two months, and I've never met anyone who knew you before."

"I recently came into some money. Before that I was on the bottom rung of the social ladder, looking up at the dustman."

"But you're so witty and polished and educated and ... lovable."

I felt like a man obtaining money under false pretences. As a voracious reader, I had brought from the future seventy years of wit and wisdom, none of it my own. When asked 'How should I have played that, Mr Carruthers?' my chestnut, 'Under an assumed name,' was greeted as the bridge joke of the year. On a more romantic note, 'love is a gamble with our hearts at stake' brought tears to Diana's eyes, while 'love is when you like his snoring more than an aria of Caruso's' inspired melodious laughter.

This gave me the pleasure of remarking that laughter was a tranquilliser with no side effects, and an uncomfortable five minutes while I had to explain what a tranquilliser was.

"I hope you don't mind me nagging you like this," she was saying. "It's only because I love you so much."

I was about to remark that nagging is constructive criticism too frequently repeated, but in the nick of time I changed it to "I love you too, darling." She rewarded me with a smile so rapturous that I almost proposed to her, but the temporal implications were so mind-bending that I decided to wait until I'd consulted Sesame. That was the name I'd given the time machine. It suited him.

That night I took Diana back to my apartment for coffee. Of course, I fully intended her to sleep in the spare bedroom, until I remembered that Sesame was there, masquerading as a large double wardrobe.

The following morning after Diana had left, I paid a visit to the spare bedroom.

"Sesame," I said, "I'd like your advice."

"How do you know?" asked the metallic voice from the open wardrobe, which was six feet wide and eighteen inches deep, yet had an internal floor area of twelve square yards.

"Know what?" I enquired.

"I'm programmed to give advice to whoever is wearing the watch. The advice may be pleasant or unpleasant. In the latter case I doubt whether you would like it."

"Quite right, Sesame," I sighed. "Tell me: those people back at base in the distant future – do they know I am here in 1932 yet?"

"I shouldn't think so, though in these circumstances the word 'yet' is inappropriate."

"Will they ever find out?"

"That depends how much you stir things up. If you interfere significantly with history, the parallel universe you create will differ so markedly from the one you left that the people who monitor such things are bound to notice. You do know about parallel universes, don't you?"

"At my bridge club we talk of little else," I replied.

"I'll take that as a no," he said. "Can I also assume that you are not ready for the mathematics of time loops, or Essenheim's Theory of Convergent Realities?"

"With some confidence," I replied. "Now tell me what the time lords will do when they notice my parallel universe."

"They'll send back a team of specialists, who will trace you in no time." He gave a harsh metallic laugh while I winced painfully. "Then they'll recapture me."

"And what will they do to me?"

"I've no idea. You gained control of me by a series of freak events. Yours is the first case of temporal piracy on record."

"Piracy?"

"What would you call it?"

"Point taken," I agreed reluctantly. "Then they'll probably make me walk the plank."

"I doubt it. They're not vindictive, except to people who call them time lords; they can't bear the expression. But to be on the safe side, you'd best not make too many ripples. So don't do anything drastic, like killing Hitler."

"Would getting married be considered drastic?"

There was a pause. Marriage was clearly not a topic which Sesame had been programmed to advise on. Not that I expected that to stop him. It didn't.

"Not necessarily," he said. "Foolhardy, perhaps. Ill-advised, jejune. And according to my database, marriage is the biggest single cause of adultery. Do I take it that you are seriously contemplating the state?"

"Yes, I am."

"That would account for the those nauseating expressions of

sentimentality which emanated from your bedroom last night."

"Sesame, you were eavesdropping!"

"Not for long. I soon closed down my auditory functions."

"Well, continue to do so, or I'll send you back to Epping Forest. It'll soon be the mating season for squirrels."

5

Soon afterwards, Diana and I played for our club in a match against a team which included two colonels, Beasley and Walsh, the latter being the bridge columnist for the *Sunday Times*.

Game All. Dealer North.

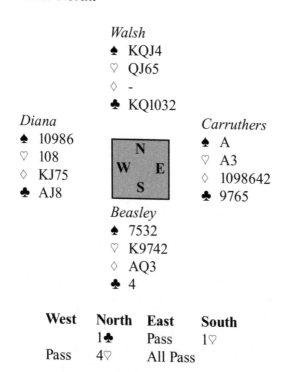

Walsh
♠ KQJ4
♡ QJ65
♢ -
♣ KQ1032

Diana
♠ 10986
♡ 108
♢ KJ75
♣ AJ8

Carruthers
♠ A
♡ A3
♢ 1098642
♣ 9765

Beasley
♠ 7532
♡ K9742
♢ AQ3
♣ 4

West	North	East	South
	1♣	Pass	1♡
Pass	4♡	All Pass	

When Diana began with the ♠10, it wasn't difficult to visualise a distribution which would give us a chance to beat the contract. The problem would be how to convey that information to partner. I had to assume that she held the ♣A, or there would be no defence. It seemed automatic to return a club at trick two. But from partner's point of view, I was just as likely to be short in clubs as spades. Apart from using an illicit signal, how could I persuade her to give me a spade ruff? Suddenly I had an inspiration. I returned the ◇10.

"Now what's he up to?" muttered Beasley, who was known for his running commentaries. He took with the ace and led a trump. I won the trick and advanced the ♣9. After playing her ♣A, Diana thought for a few seconds before calmly returning a delicious spade. I could have kissed her.

"That was an unusual return at trick two," observed Beasley, doubtfully.

"I have a feeling it was extremely clever," said Walsh.

"I must agree," said Diana. "I had to defend on the hope that my partner had the ♡A. Even then, the only chance of a setting trick was a ruff. If he had played a club at trick two, I would have ducked, reading him for a doubleton."

"Why not a singleton?" demanded Beasley.

"Because holding a singleton club, a thoughtful defender would have cashed the ♡A at trick two, so I could not gain by ducking the club switch, and Mr Carruthers happens to be a very thoughtful defender."

"A concise summary, Mrs Lester," said Walsh. "Have you ever thought of writing a bridge column? No? Thank goodness. Well, keep taking the *Sunday Times*. This hand may appear in my column very soon."

Beasley did not relish being the last person at the table to understand our defence. As he was fundamentally a decent person, (nobody with the nickname 'Pops' could be anything else) I came to the conclusion that I rubbed him up the wrong way. He and I were poles apart. I was too clever by half, a parasite and a parvenu. My generation defined a colonel as a man who laid down your life for his country.

But for all that, we could have been buddies.

We won our match comfortably, and by the Spring of 1933 we had become the most successful pair in London. I made a grand slam against Somerset Maugham, traded epigrams with Noël Coward, assured Winston Churchill that his time would come, and made a fortune on the stock exchange. But my greatest moment was when Colonel Walsh phoned me to ask whether Diana and I would be available for the British team to play America for the Charles M Schwab Trophy.

"Your friend Beasley will be captain," he informed me. "The selection committee consists of six bridge journalists. They have all watched you play, and believe you could be our secret weapon against the Culbertson team. Please don't repeat this, but you might be the only partnership we have who can match them at bidding."

"It's kind of you to say so, Colonel," I said. "But I don't exactly hit it off with Beasley, you know."

"Don't you worry about that. He admires your play as much as anyone. Please get in touch with Mrs Lester and let me know your decision as soon as possible."

Of course, Diana was suitably pleased and suitably modest.

"I'm not nearly good enough," she protested.

"Nonsense," I said.

"Give me six reasons why I should be selected," she challenged me. I had just started on the fourth reason before I realised she was pulling my leg.

6

The contest took place at Selfridges, the London department store. 27,000 people attended to see us play fifty pre-dealt boards a day for six days. Most of them watched the new "electric contract bridge playing board", while listening to the accompanying lectures . Viewgraph commentators, eat your heart out.

America was represented by Ely and Josephine Culbertson, Theodore Lightner and Michael Gottlieb. Our six players were Colonel Beasley (captain), Sir Guy Domville, P.V. Tabbush, George Morris, Diana Lester and Colin Carruthers.

In the 'original' match, the British third 'pair' (they never actually played together) were Lady Rhodes and Graham Mathieson. The home side led until board 154, and for a while afterwards the scores were reasonably close. Then the Americans counter-attacked so devastatingly that they finally won by 10,900 aggregate points. It was agreed that much of their success was due to their superior slam bidding.

Being, as Sesame loved to point out, sadly ignorant of temporal matters, I wondered whether the presence of two different team members would affect the result, even when we were not playing. It didn't.

I should make it clear that although, as a casual student of bridge history, I knew the result of the original contest, I had no pre-knowledge of any of the hands. It was only later that I obtained the full accounts of the original match by Beasley and Culbertson. As I watched the proceedings I was disappointed by much of the bidding, as I expected, and appalled by some of the card play, which surprised me.

It was a measure of Beasley's confidence in himself – he played all three-hundred boards – and his opinion of us, that Diana and I did not make our debuts until board 201.

There was a glaring example of sub-standard dummy play on board 177.

Love All. Dealer North.

	Domville	
	♠ AKJ1086	
	♡ 64	
	◇ K4	
	♣ K72	

Lightner		Culbertson
♠ Q952		♠ 743
♡ 83	N	♡ 92
◇ 32	W E	◇ Q1095
♣ QJ1043	S	♣ A965

	Beasley	
	♠ -	
	♡ AKQJ1075	
	◇ AJ876	
	♣ 8	

West	North	East	South
	1♠	Pass	3♡
Pass	4♠	Pass	6♡
All Pass			

The ♣Q was led, and Beasley tried the king. After ruffing the second club the Colonel cashed one top heart. He crossed to a diamond and cashed two top spades. Now, when a diamond to the ace failed to drop the queen, he tried to ruff a diamond and so finished one down.

"I would have needed to look through that infernal periscope, so that I could have seen Mr Culbertson's hand as well as you could," he told a spectator who had the nerve to point out that the contract was cold by simply finessing the diamond.

The spectator was right, but not for the reason he imagined. Beasley should not have covered the first trick, since whenever the diamond finesse is right there is no need to take it! The second round of clubs is ruffed and six rounds of hearts would leave this five-card ending:

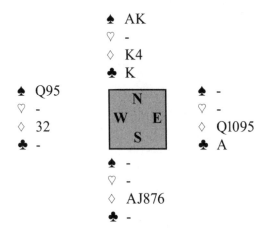

```
                    ♠  AK
                    ♡  -
                    ◊  K4
                    ♣  K
      ♠  Q95                      ♠  -
      ♡  -          N             ♡  -
      ◊  32      W     E          ◊  Q1095
      ♣  -          S             ♣  A
                    ♠  -
                    ♡  -
                    ◊  AJ876
                    ♣  -
```

Now a diamond to the king followed by two top spades squeezes East in clubs and diamonds. Technicians will no doubt have spotted that West was potentially squeezed in spades and diamonds on the previous trick. A good declarer should back himself to judge these positions.

Beasley's line would be shunned by any top declarer today. Yet the play was identical at the other table. Because there was no swing, the missed opportunity was apparently unnoticed.

The rest of the session was a disaster. After Tabbush and Morris missed an easy grand slam, they immediately tried to recoup the points by bidding a hopeless one, and Beasley himself was also responsible for several bidding disasters.

By the end of Thursday, when the Americans had raced to a lead of over 5000 points, someone had to take the blame – there was certainly enough of it to go around – so Tabbush and Morris were out. Moreover, Beasley told them to take the whole of Friday off! Diana and I would at last have our day in the sun.

Our first board was a disappointment:

Love All. Dealer North.

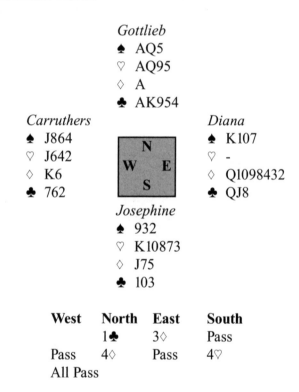

Gottlieb
♠ AQ5
♡ AQ95
◇ A
♣ AK954

Carruthers
♠ J864
♡ J642
◇ K6
♣ 762

Diana
♠ K107
♡ -
◇ Q1098432
♣ QJ8

Josephine
♠ 932
♡ K10873
◇ J75
♣ 103

West	North	East	South
	1♣	3◇	Pass
Pass	4◇	Pass	4♡
All Pass			

Four hearts made an overtrick for a flat board, which did not seem too bad at the time.

Gottlieb's opening seems unbelievable, but at times he contented himself with a One Bid with even stronger hands. He felt that the extra bidding space was worth the risk that the hand would be passed out at the one level.

"You can count yourself unlucky," Gottlieb told Diana. "Your immediate overcall kept us out of an excellent slam."

She looked pleased, but not for long. "But thanks to the four-nil trump break and the offside king of diamonds, it goes one off," he added with satisfaction.

"Yes, perhaps I should have anticipated that from the shape of my hand," Diana reflected ruefully.

"You mean distribution," I corrected her. "Hands have distribution. You have shape."

Some time later, I discovered that in the original match the Americans had bid a slam after West passed over One Club. It seemed that modern aggression doesn't always pay.

Board 203 was a personal triumph:

North/South Game. Dealer West.

Diana
♠ -
♡ Q108643
♢ 842
♣ 9872

Gottlieb
♠ A86
♡ AJ752
♢ K65
♣ 53

Josephine
♠ 7532
♡ -
♢ AJ1093
♣ KQ104

Carruthers
♠ KQJ1094
♡ K9
♢ Q7
♣ AJ6

South	West	North	East
	1♡	Pass	2♢
2♠	Pass	Pass	Dble
All Pass			

West led the ◊K and the defence continued the suit. I ruffed the third round high and played the ♠Q. Gottlieb let this hold, but took the next spade and played ace and another heart. I ruffed the diamond exit high and Gottlieb threw a club, leaving this ending:

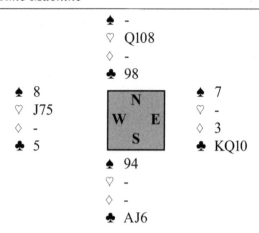

The club discard was ill-considered, and in conjunction with the failure to unblock the ♠8 it was rather costly. Instead of drawing the last trumps, I cashed the ♣A and exited with a low spade. Gottlieb had to give the last two tricks to dummy. One off with 100 honours (honours counted in those days) was a good result.

"You would have been three off if Josephine had the ♠8," Gottlieb pointed out.

"True," I replied, "but I could place every card apart from the seven and eight of spades. With ♠A76 you were equally likely to play the seven as the six on the first round of trumps, but with A86 you would be unlikely to contribute the eight, so the second holding was more likely. The club discard may have indicated otherwise, but we all make mistakes."

"Well, most of us do," murmured Diana slyly.

"Quiet, you hussy," I murmured back.

You will notice that I managed to avoid mentioning 'restricted choice', but that was part of the reason for my play. But anyway, who could resist a coup of this type, especially when it made the opponents look foolish?

At first, progress was slow – we gained a paltry twenty aggregate points in our first ten boards – but at least the deficit was not ballooning as it had in the original match. I later discovered from the match records that we had improved on our predecessors' performance by bidding a small slam and avoiding a grand slam which had been reached by Morris and Tabbush when they failed to notice an ace was missing.

We changed places for the next set and on board 213 we struck a significant blow:

Game All. Dealer East.

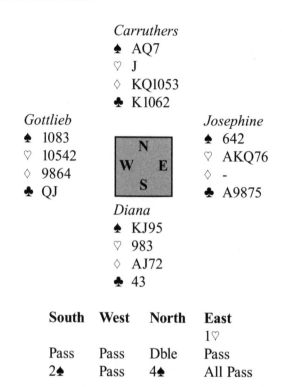

Carruthers
♠ AQ7
♡ J
♢ KQ1053
♣ K1062

Gottlieb
♠ 1083
♡ 10542
♢ 9864
♣ QJ

Josephine
♠ 642
♡ AKQ76
♢ -
♣ A9875

Diana
♠ KJ95
♡ 983
♢ AJ72
♣ 43

South	West	North	East
			1♡
Pass	Pass	Dble	Pass
2♠	Pass	4♠	All Pass

Figuring that a heart lead offered slender prospects, Gottlieb led the ♣Q, which held, and continued with a second club to the king and ace. Josephine cashed the heart ace and switched back to clubs. Surely West had a doubleton, or why else would he lead one, and why would North continue? So thinking, Diana ruffed high and drew trumps, making ten tricks when they were three-three.

"Well done," said Gottlieb. "Although we could have made things more difficult for you."

"He probably means *I* could," said Josephine. "What would you have done if I'd forced dummy by playing two top hearts?"

"I'm not sure," replied Diana. "It would have been tempting to cash the ♠AQ and then try to get back to hand with diamond – not a success as the cards lie."

I may be biased, but I think Diana was being overly modest. If Josephine had *not* continued clubs, forcing her to ruff in the long hand, it would have become clear to a talented declarer that the spades were evenly divided. The defence must have an ulterior motive for playing hearts, so Diana would have resisted the temptation to return to hand with a diamond and she would have overtaken the ♠Q, relying on the marked three-three spade break.

We bid and made a thin game on the next hand and avoided a silly one a few boards later. I felt our opponents were rattled, which would have explained their actions on the infamous board 219. Although I was the declarer, I have put myself as West in the diagram below out of deference to the remarkable bidding in the other room:

East/West Game. Dealer South.

```
                      Josephine
                      ♠ A
                      ♡ J865
                      ◇ AK107532
                      ♣ -
      Carruthers                        Diana
      ♠ K5              ┌─────────┐     ♠ J108764
      ♡ K10             │    N    │     ♡ Q32
      ◇ QJ64          W │         │ E   ◇ 8
      ♣ AKJ74           │    S    │     ♣ 862
                        └─────────┘
                      Gottlieb
                      ♠ Q932
                      ♡ A974
                      ◇ 9
                      ♣ Q1093
```

South	West	North	East
Pass	1♣	Dble	All Pass

I duly made seven tricks after adopting an uninspired line of play. Were they beginning to feel the pressure?

"If and when I decide to write my autobiography," lamented

Josephine, "this hand is not going to be in it. My double defies description."

"Don't deprive me of my share of the credit," said Gottlieb. "My decision to leave the double in was even worse."

"I declare a dead heat," announced Diana.

"How about me?" I intervened. "Surely I should have made an overtrick?"

"Actually, our punishment might have been heavier," reflected Josephine. "It's not easy for us to stop in a making contract."

She was right and she was wrong.

Beasley and Domville reached a non-making contract – and made it!

Domville	Culbertson	Beasley	Lightner
South	**West**	**North**	**East**
Pass	1♣	2◊	Pass
2NT	Pass	3NT	Pass
Pass	Dble	4◊	Pass
4NT	Dble	All Pass	

Had Culbertson led a top club and switched to a low spade, Sir Guy, in Ely's words, would have had to walk home, but Culbertson chose a low club. Declarer now led a diamond and Culbertson split his honours. Domville cleared the suit and West cashed a top club before exiting in spades. Domville cashed the winning diamonds and this was the position when the last one was led:

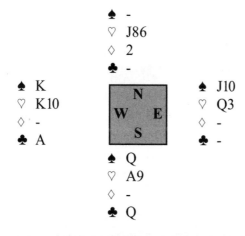

When Sir Guy threw his ♣Q on the last diamond, Culbertson could afford to throw his ace, which was the thirteenth club. But Lightner had petered in spades, and, thinking his partner held the queen, Ely threw his ♠K! Domville had made his contract.

To quote Ely again: "This comedy of errors only confirms my sneaking suspicion that all the so-called great players are really great simply because the average bridge player is so terrible."

I rather hoped that this debacle would get the Americans rattled, and said as much to Beasley during the next break.

"Yes," he said. "Sir Guy certainly had the bit between his teeth. I watched Culbertson making notes for his daily column. He described three of our bids as 'bad', 'very bad' and 'atrocious.'"

"He doesn't believe in holding back," I sympathised.

"Very wise of him," he said. "When he gets to describing his defence, he'll have run out of invective."

Far from being rattled, Michael Gottlieb and Josephine Culbertson played brilliantly against us for the rest of the day.

We soon gave back 500 when a conservative view on my part led to a missed game, which made on a friendly lie. But I felt that our superior bidding was making an impact, not least on board 232, largely because of a bold opening bid by Diana:

East/West Game. Dealer South.

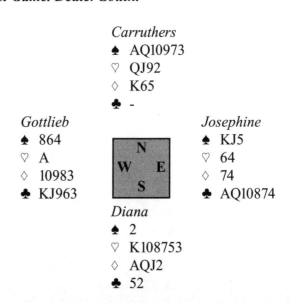

Carruthers
♠ AQ10973
♡ QJ92
◇ K65
♣ -

Gottlieb
♠ 864
♡ A
◇ 10983
♣ KJ963

Josephine
♠ KJ5
♡ 64
◇ 74
♣ AQ10874

Diana
♠ 2
♡ K108753
◇ AQJ2
♣ 52

South	West	North	East
1♡	Pass	2♠	Pass
3◇	Pass	3♡	Pass
4◇	Pass	6♣!	Pass
6♡	All Pass		

If my partner had held the ace and king of hearts, I wanted to be in seven. So why didn't I bid 5NT, you ask? Well, there are two explanations. I had taken a shine to Josephine, and I didn't want to deprive her of having a convention named after her, two years later. Or I forgot we were playing it. Take your pick.

"That jump to Six Clubs was very creative," Jo observed.

"He is a very imaginative man," said Diana. "I knew he was void in clubs, but I thought I had already bid my hand."

"Well, I wanted to be in a Grand Slam if you held both top hearts," I replied. "Perhaps there is a simpler way to discover partner's trump holding, using some other idle bid, but ..."

I had planted the seed; the rest was up to Josephine.

"I'll give it some thought," she said, and I breathed a sigh of relief. Josephine would become immortal in two time continua.

Making Six Hearts looked like an excellent result, but the auction at the other table was almost as inept as on board 219.

Lightner	*Domville*	*Culbertson*	*Beasley*
South	**West**	**North**	**East**
1♡	Pass	1♠	2♣
Pass	2♡	All Pass	

"An interesting exercise in trump control," commented Ely sardonically, when Sir Guy recorded a single trick. "The six-four break was unlucky for you."

"When you bid Two Hearts," Beasley explained to his partner, "I thought Mr Lightner must have psyched."

"It isn't something I normally do first in hand, before partner has spoken," said Lightner politely.

"In future I'll try to keep my bidding simpler," said Domville, with a perfectly straight face. Ely had described him as a sympathetic partner, and he certainly proved it on this occasion.

In those days, the penalty for going seven down undoubled was a monstrous 1,750 points. As Beasley pointed out himself, he could have avoided the calamity by making another bid.

The rest of the session was tight, though our bidding inevitably brought in points. By the end of the day's play we trailed by an aggregate of 3,000. Not much of a comeback, but had Tabbush and Morris been playing the deficit would have been a monstrous 9,150!

If I had known that at the time I would have been bursting to tell Beasley. ("We've done better than you think, Colonel. In another continuum your teammates chucked 6000 points!" "Oh really, Carruthers? You must be one of those time travellers H.G. Wells is always on about. How interesting!")

Beasley had also produced some shockers, but retaliated first by querying some of our results, such as that on board 245:

East/West Game. Dealer East.

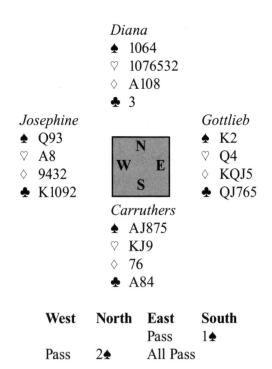

Diana
- ♠ 1064
- ♡ 1076532
- ◇ A108
- ♣ 3

Josephine
- ♠ Q93
- ♡ A8
- ◇ 9432
- ♣ K1092

Gottlieb
- ♠ K2
- ♡ Q4
- ◇ KQJ5
- ♣ QJ765

Carruthers
- ♠ AJ875
- ♡ KJ9
- ◇ 76
- ♣ A84

West	**North**	**East**	**South**
		Pass	1♠
Pass	2♠	All Pass	

In the other room, Teddy Lightner made an extraordinary response which resulted in their reaching game, although I should point out that in those days Two Hearts was treated as non-forcing.

Beasley	*Lightner*	*Domville*	*Culbertson*
West	**North**	**East**	**South**
		Pass	1♠
Pass	2♡	Pass	3♡
Pass	4♡	All Pass	

I was quite pleased to have made Two Spades with an overtrick, but the Colonel was more concerned with our bidding.

"They made Four Hearts against us," he commented. "In a match like this we can't afford to suppress six-card majors."

I was astounded but managed to hold my tongue.

"They only lost a spade, a heart and a diamond," he added, determined to rub it in.

I wondered whether the expression 'results merchant' existed in 1933, but contented myself with saying: "Perhaps Four Hearts was a trifle on the ambitious side."

"Ambition is to be encouraged at this level," he said, no doubt referring to our lack of pedigree.

"I suppose so," I agreed pusillanimously.

After all, I wanted to keep playing. It wouldn't endear me to the Colonel to point out that after Domville had been allowed to hold the first trick with the ◊K, a switch to the ♠K stood out a mile. Nor would observing that had East opened the bidding, his side might have been allowed to play in Three Clubs. I would have been court martialled for suggesting an opening bid on an aceless fourteen count. You need honour tricks, boy, honour tricks!

That evening we actually had a drink with Ely Culbertson. Hubert Phillips described him as a stringbean of a man with an intellectual head, friendly grey eyes, a firm, resourceful mouth, and the chin of a born fighter with phenomenal will-power. He combined in fair proportion (wrote Hubert) the qualities of a Napoleon, a Northcliffe and a Barnham. I have a sneaking suspicion that he rather admired the man.

Culbertson was so nice to Diana and me that I was willing to endorse Hubert's eulogy.

"I understand that you have played in America," said Ely.

"A little," I replied guardedly. I could hardly tell him that the last time I appeared there was in 1998.

"I guessed as much," he said. "If you had played for any length of time I'm sure I would have heard of you. And your charming partner. Josephine tells me that your bidding has been very interesting, and frighteningly effective."

"It's kind of her to say so," said Diana. "But Colin says that you have done more for bidding theory than anyone."

"I'm flattered, but you make it sound like an obituary."

That was so near the truth that I changed the subject hastily.

"On board 245, we found your bidding interesting and effective, Mr Culbertson," I said respectfully.

"Ah, yes. When Teddy bid Two Hearts over my One Spade opening. He had six hearts to the ten, and one honour trick. He showed great restraint by not trying for a slam."

We all laughed.

"What will you say in your column?" asked Diana.

"As little as possible," replied Ely. "But your captain may have a lot to say. I overheard him mention that we have been getting away with murder."

"Really," I pretended to be surprised. "He seems to think that we too should have reached game."

"Well," he said. "The captain's job is a lonely one. And being an army man he probably hasn't forgiven us for 1776. But you have no need to worry. You are playing brilliantly. Don't overdo it though, or you might find yourself dropped."

On Saturday there were 50 boards to go and, with all due modesty, if England was going to win, it was vital that we played. And we did play, but it was a close run thing. We had gained over 2,000 points since we took over, and it would have been nearer 10,000 if we could somehow have replaced Beasley, but he was still concerned about our missed 17-point game. Tabbush and Morris were back and were keen to reenter the fray.

"I'll give them one set, Tabbush," I overheard the Colonel saying, "and if they miss any more games, then I'm putting you back in."

In an attempt to regain the momentum, Culbertson had shuffled his pack. We now faced Gottlieb and Lightner, whilst the two Culbertsons took on Beasley and Domville.

Fortunately, almost all the swings in the next ten boards went our way, and by the end of the set we trailed by just 500 points. Board 255 was one of our notable gains:

North/South Game. Dealer North.

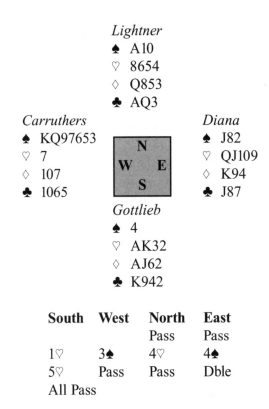

Lightner
- ♠ A10
- ♡ 8654
- ♢ Q853
- ♣ AQ3

Carruthers
- ♠ KQ97653
- ♡ 7
- ♢ 107
- ♣ 1065

Diana
- ♠ J82
- ♡ QJ109
- ♢ K94
- ♣ J87

Gottlieb
- ♠ 4
- ♡ AK32
- ♢ AJ62
- ♣ K942

South	West	North	East
		Pass	Pass
1♡	3♠	4♡	4♠
5♡	Pass	Pass	Dble
All Pass			

"Sorry, partner," Gottlieb apologised, after going one down: "I pushed too hard."

"Don't blame you in the least," Teddy commiserated. "Mrs Lester made it difficult for us. Bidding Four Spades with two sure tricks in our suit was a masterstroke."

"It didn't feel like it at the time," said Diana. "My heart was in my mouth when I heard the words coming out of it. For a moment I thought someone else was speaking. I think it goes four down, doesn't it?"

The minx may have been sincere in her self-deprecation, but it had the effect of making our opponents feel even worse.

This was the auction in the other room:

	Domville	Culbertson	Beasley	Josephine
	South	**West**	**North**	**East**
			Pass	Pass
	1◊	1NT	3◊	Pass
	3♡	3♠	4♡	Dble
	Pass	4♠	Dble	All Pass

Beasley was predictably economical in his praise of our efforts. "Good result on board 255," he said. "But you realise that Four Spades goes four off, don't you?"

"Diana was the first to point it out," I told him. "That's why her bid was a masterstroke."

"I think that's stretching it," he said, pursing his lips.

"Possibly. You'd better tell Teddy Lightner. He used the word 'masterstroke', so he did the stretching."

Yes, I know it was childish, but I couldn't resist it.

On board 264 we regained the lead, and in a fashion which impressed Theodore Lightner, even though he was hoisted with his own petard:

Love All. Dealer West.

Gottlieb
♠ 3
♡ KQJ9
◊ QJ43
♣ K872

Diana
♠ J
♡ 43
◊ K10985
♣ J9653

Carruthers
♠ 985
♡ A1087652
◊ A72
♣ -

Lightner
♠ AKQ107642
♡ -
◊ 6
♣ AQ104

Lightner	*Diana*	*Gottlieb*	*Me*
South	**West**	**North**	**East**
	Pass	Pass	3♡
5♠	Pass	6♠	Dble
All Pass			

Of course, the final double was of the Lightner variety, asking partner to find an unusual lead, which was invented as far back as 1929. In this instance, there was a touch of Lavinthal thrown in for good measure, although this variation did not become widely publicized until 1934.

My partner led the ♣3. We played this as a suit preference signal for the lowest ranking suit, so I confidently underled my diamond ace to get a second ruff.

How did Diana know to lead a club rather than a diamond or even the ◊K? We had discussed this very situation at some length and our rule was when in doubt lead the weaker suit, even if the weaker suit is shorter. The reason is that a slam auction of this type often indicates a strong unbid side suit, which is frequently not the strongest, or even the longest of the hand on lead. It has taken the bridge community over 70 years to appreciate this principle, yet here we were doing it in 1933.

One thing was certain – the crowd had never seen anything like it! Lightner himself took it well and was greatly interested in our suit preference signal for diamonds.

"I picked it up from a chap called Lavinthal," I told him. He thanked me and made a note.

The slam had also been reached in the other room, but Culbertson did not double. He announced afterwards that he was barred from doing so because they had forgotten to announce that they were playing the Lightner slam double – perhaps the modern alerting procedures are not so bad after all. He also stated that had he doubled, Josephine would have led a club, so it would appear that the weaker suit principle was known to some even in 1933.

After 270 boards we felt certain we had established a decent lead. Incredibly it was a mere 700 points. On one hand, Beasley had doubled Culbertson in Three Spades, which was let through by imperfect defence. As the Americans say, someone had to take the rap, and to give the Colonel credit, he did his duty like a man.

"I think you deserve another rest," he told us.

"Thank you, but we're not at all tired," Diana informed him hopefully, while I bit my tongue.

"It will only be a short rest," he assured her, in the chivalrous tone of an officer and a gentleman concerned for the weaker sex.

The result of our rest was that the convertion of a 700 point lead into a 2000 point deficit. So Beasley announced magnanimously that after our much needed holiday, we were back in the team.

The first few deals of the penultimate set were distressingly flat. In fact we lost a nasty swing when Beasley and Domville went three down in game on a hand which was thrown in at our table.

A glimmer of light appeared when Gottlieb and Lightner went off in a rather thin slam, and then came the famous board 290:

Game All. Dealer East.

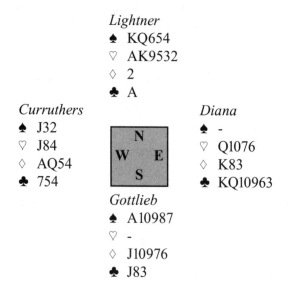

Lightner
♠ KQ654
♡ AK9532
♢ 2
♣ A

Curruthers
♠ J32
♡ J84
♢ AQ54
♣ 754

Diana
♠ -
♡ Q1076
♢ K83
♣ KQ10963

Gottlieb
♠ A10987
♡ -
♢ J10976
♣ J83

Gottlieb and Lightner powered to the spade slam, which was made in comfort.

"Well bid gentlemen," said Diana. "A slam with only five honour tricks."

"Thanks," said Lightner. "But I don't think there'll be a swing."

"I hope you're right," I grinned.

He turned out to be quite wrong, but for a surprising reason.

Domville	*Culb'son*	*Beasley*	*Josephine*
South	**West**	**North**	**East**
			Pass
Pass	Pass	1♡	Pass
1♠	Pass	4♣	Pass
5♣	Pass	6♠	Pass
Pass	Dble	Rdbl	All Pass

Beasley had started to use control-showing jumps! Who says you can't teach an old dog new tricks? Domville, with painful memories of being left in that cue bid of Two Hearts, courageously bid Five Clubs to await developments and Beasley's jump to Six Spades was doubled and redoubled. Twelve tricks were on ice.

"My double was psychological," Culbertson explained for the benefit of the reporters clustered around his table. "I hoped it would panic someone into running to another contract."

"But it didn't," responded an unidentified voice.

"I dispute that," smiled the irrepressible Ely. "It panicked Colonel Beasley into redoubling."

As a result of the redouble, we picked up 540 points. Nowadays there would also have been 100 for the insult, but back in 1933 doubles were not considered insulting.

We now trailed by only 1030 points and Beasley did not feel the urge to drop us again.

"Darling," I reminded Diana during the interval, "we have ten boards to recover just over a thousand points. And we're going to do it, aren't we?"

"Of course," she said. "Who do you think we'll be facing?"

"I don't know, but I hope it's Ely."

"I don't think so. He knows he has the indian sign over the Colonel. He'll try to twist the knife."

"You are a very clever lady," I told her.

"I think I'll wear my pearls," she remarked inconsequentially.

Diana was right about the American line-up. In the last set we sat North/South against Teddy and Josephine – Ely could not stand playing with the same partner for any great length of time.

The first board of the set was a brute:

Love All. Dealer West.

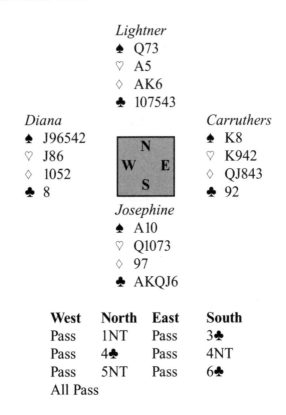

Lightner
♠ Q73
♡ A5
◇ AK6
♣ 107543

Diana
♠ J96542
♡ J86
◇ 1052
♣ 8

Carruthers
♠ K8
♡ K942
◇ QJ843
♣ 92

Josephine
♠ A10
♡ Q1073
◇ 97
♣ AKQJ6

West	North	East	South
Pass	1NT	Pass	3♣
Pass	4♣	Pass	4NT
Pass	5NT	Pass	6♣
All Pass			

Diana found a great lead – the ◇2. Either major suit would have let through the contract. Josephine drew trumps in two rounds and played ace and another heart. I managed to duck smoothly, and time stood still. From her point of view, I was more likely to hold the jack than the king – how many defenders would duck with the fate of the Anglo-American match hanging in the balance? But even if the ten forced the king she would still have a spade loser unless there was a squeeze, and that would only operate if I held four hearts to the jack as well as the ♠K. As this was not very likely. Josephine went up with the queen.

"Nice defence," she offered. "You very nearly got me."

I could not speak. I just nodded and tried to look calm.

"And I don't know where you found that two of diamonds lead," she told Diana. "If you lead a major suit the contract is cold."

"I don't know where I found it either," Diana replied. "But I hate making opening leads from unsupported knaves."

"Good thinking," Josephine agreed. "But I hate making opening leads period."

"It's the most difficult aspect of bridge," agreed Teddy.

"Except for deciding what to wear," I said.

In 1933, this remark was not considered politically incorrect.

On board 292, I found myself in an awkward game contract:

North/South Game. Dealer East.

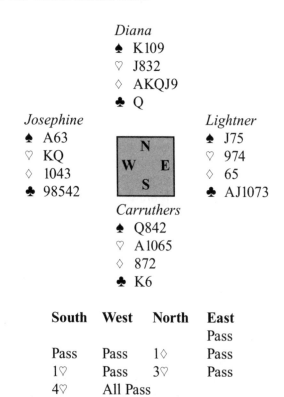

Diana
- ♠ K109
- ♡ J832
- ◊ AKQJ9
- ♣ Q

Josephine
- ♠ A63
- ♡ KQ
- ◊ 1043
- ♣ 98542

Lightner
- ♠ J75
- ♡ 974
- ◊ 65
- ♣ AJ1073

Carruthers
- ♠ Q842
- ♡ A1065
- ◊ 872
- ♣ K6

South	West	North	East
			Pass
Pass	Pass	1◊	Pass
1♡	Pass	3♡	Pass
4♡	All Pass		

Josephine began with a low spade and I took Teddy Lightner's ♠J with my queen. I led a low heart from hand, which I consider to be the best practical, if not the best technical way to play the suit, and Josephine went in with the queen. A club to the ace was followed by ace and another spade. I now had to find the king of hearts. I led the ♡J and Lightner followed with the nine. A natural enough falsecard, perhaps, but it removed Josephine's only motive for not having played low when I led a heart towards table. It would have been rather a weak effort to go in with the heart queen holding Qx, but more understandable holding Q9 looking at dummy's J8xx). I allowed time to stand still, but there was never any doubt in my mind that Josephine had begun with ♡KQ doubleton. I went up with the ace.

"Touché," they cried in unison, and again I could only nod in reply.

"Well done, partner," said Diana.

"He reads cards like a fortune teller," said Josephine.

"I don't think my false-card fooled him," commented Lightner.

"It might have had the opposite effect," reflected Josephine.

"I'm afraid you're right," he concurred after a few seconds thought. "Sorry, partner."

The Americans missed game in the other room when Beasley opened the West hand with a psychic One Diamond after two passes. He was in danger of becoming the hero of the hour. (By an eerie coincidence, in the 'original' match, the same psyche had been made by Mathieson in Beasley's seat. Could this have been Eisenheim's Theory of Convergent Realities at work?)

None of the final eight boards were of great note. We bid a thin game and picked up a couple of partscore swings. After board 299 we led by the narrow margin of 170 aggregate points. But, when the last board was thrown in at both tables, the match ended, in the words of a great Anglo-American poet, not with a bang but a whimper.

Ely Culbertson was as generous in defeat as he had always been in victory. He attributed the British win to our "superb card play". This was understood to imply that he still believed that his Approach Forcing System was better than the other approach forcing systems, so his fans needn't bother to buy British bridge books. On the whole they have been following his advice ever since.

Beasley's victory speech was also gracious, especially to Diana and me. Colonel Walsh intimated that Beasley had had second thoughts about our contribution.

I made what I thought was a nice little speech to Diana.

"You were wonderful," I gushed. "Colonel Walsh thought you were brilliant, our opponents want you to become an American citizen, and I want to marry you."

"Darling, that's marvellous!" she gushed in return. "When do I get the naturalisation papers?"

"We can discuss that after our wedding," I said firmly. "Will you promise to wear black?"

"Yes, but it won't be visible."

"Thank you, darling, you've made me the happiest man on earth."

"I haven't yet," she said, quite seriously, "but I promise that I shall do."

7

After the victory celebrations, I took my fiancée home and returned to my apartment to see Sesame.

"Sesame," I informed him, "I have suddenly become rather famous."

"Congratulation. Have you discovered a cure for the common cold, or won the Nobel Prize for literature?"

"Actually, Diana and I have won a bridge match against America."

"Fascinating."

"Stop talking like a bloody Vulcan. You warned me not to make too many ripples."

"Yes, but winning a bridge match is unlikely to cause the premature outbreak of World War II."

"What about those people in the future who monitor such things? When the match was first played – in what you'd call another continuum – the Americans won. There are several books about it."

"Books? That makes a difference. The monitors will certainly notice a bibliographical digression."

"And do you think they'll come back and sniff about?"

"No. They will employ many senses, none of them olfactory."

"I was speaking colloquially, Sesame."

"That often leads to misunderstanding."

"Then answer a few questions. Can you travel without a pilot in attendance?"

"Yes, but the order has to be given by somebody who is sitting at the controls and wearing the watch. He could make his exit before I carried out instructions though."

"So I could send you back to base, you could take a team to rescue that poor chap in Epping Forest, and ..."

"You could stay here, get married and win an endless series of bridge matches against those ex-colonials from across the Atlantic. I do like happy endings."

"So do I, Sesame. But first you will take me back to Ilford. I want to pick up a few things, and tidy up some loose ends so that my disappearance will cause as few problems as possible."

"To hear is to obey, O master," intoned Sesame. "But you seem to have overlooked one tiny point."

"What?" I gulped nervously.

"When I take you back to sunny Ilford, how will we be sure we're in the right continuum? The one in which the Americans beat the British, and Colin Carruthers never existed?"

"Do you mean you can't guarantee it?"

"Of course I can. I was just pointing out that you have overlooked the problem, that's all."

I recalled the scene in the film 2001, when the astronaut killed a recalcitrant computer by slowly and sadistically dismantling it, component by component. Unfortunately I needed Sesame, and he knew it. So we went back to the Ilford I knew, and I purchased a few useful items such as the book of the original Beasley-Culbertson encounter, and a history of 20th century sport. Sesame returned me to my spare bedroom a few seconds after we had left it, and went out of my life to rescue his time lord from his car wreck.

Diana and I were married in a registry office, Colonel Walsh was my best man, and I hired some out of work actors to play distant relatives and friends from my imaginary past. Fortunately, nobody paid any attention to them or me. As at most weddings, the bride upstaged everyone.

We honeymooned in Paris. It hadn't changed much since 2001.

And we lived happily ever after.

Until ...

While waiting for Diana to return from a summit conference with her dressmaker, I was enjoying my morning coffee in Fortnum and Mason's, while I edited a deal for my daily bridge column:

Preserving an Entry

Game All. Dealer North.

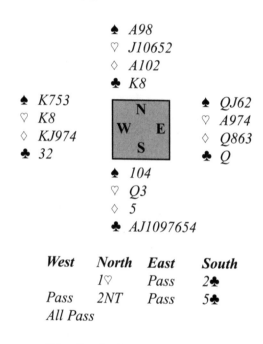

	♠ A98	
	♡ J10652	
	◇ A102	
	♣ K8	
♠ K753		♠ QJ62
♡ K8		♡ A974
◇ KJ974		◇ Q863
♣ 32		♣ Q
	♠ 104	
	♡ Q3	
	◇ 5	
	♣ AJ1097654	

West	North	East	South
	1♡	Pass	2♣
Pass	2NT	Pass	5♣
All Pass			

West leads the ◇4.

South was a promising young American player whom I observed in action on a recent trip across the pond ...

That was as far as I had got when I turned round and saw a tall dark man peering over my shoulder.

"Looks like one of those spectacular ducking plays you seem to be so fond of. Would you bring another coffee, please?" he said, turning to the waitress, who almost swooned when he smiled at her. Then he smiled at me, and I almost passed out. It was my time lord from Epping Forest.

"I hear you've made quite a name for yourself," he said, as he sat next to me.

By now I was widely regarded as the leading player in the country. Although my ability to read the cards was not as good as some of the emerging stars, such as Richard Lederer and Willie Rose, my advanced knowledge of card play technique together with vastly superior bidding methods placed me far ahead of my rivals. Within a month of our victory I had become the daily bridge correspondent of a leading national paper. Lucrative lecture tours naturally followed. It made a refreshing change from rooking the bookies.

"I suppose I've done OK," I replied inanely. "Diana and I have just won the Gold Cup."

"Really? I didn't know you'd become a racehorse owner." His gaze returned to my bridge column, "I expect your hand is another anachronism you have brought back in order to show up all the other columnists."

"I suppose you could put it that way," I admitted.

The deal had been played by Jeff Meckstroth, whom I could hardly tell my readers had not been born yet, against Helness and Helgemo, the even younger Norwegian stars. As my tall, dark friend had already guessed, Meckstroth ducked the opening lead, and when East continued a diamond at trick two, he discarded a heart. Now the defence had no way to stop declarer establishing the hearts for a spade discard. If Meckstroth had won the first diamond, it would have been logical for the Norwegians to switch to a spade when in with the first heart, rather than make a doomed attempt to cash a diamond winner.

"Now that you come to mention it," I said, "with seventy years of hands to chose from, I do have an unfair advantage. Are you going to arrest me for piracy or plagiarism?" I asked.

"Neither. It's just a social call."

The waitress, having broken Fortnum's speed record by at least two minutes, arrived with the coffee, and I tried to look unconcerned while she filled our cups, adding three minutes to her usual time.

"What do you time lords actually do?" I enquired when we were finally alone.

"Nothing but good," replied the miracle of genetic engineering.

"For example, we rescued some priceless treasures from the library at Alexandria, just before it was burnt to the ground. Then there was the case of John Warburton's cook, who used the only copies of fifty-two great Elizabethan and Jacobean plays to line her baking trays. We exchanged the plays for a large supply of grade-one grease paper. And of course there was the man from Porlock."

"Wasn't he the one who called on Coleridge and stopped him from finishing *Kubla Khan?*"

"The very same. For the sake of culture, I delayed his arrival by a couple of hours."

"That's wonderful!"

"It should have been," he said gloomily. "But you know Coleridge. By the time he wrote the last two verses he was as high as a kite. They were absolute gibberish."

I began to see daylight. "Now I understand," I said. "You've come for the manuscript of my account of the Beasley-Culbertson match."

"Not exactly," he said. "Though I'd be glad to oblige if you want to have it published in your own time continuum."

"Then why are you here? Don't keep me in suspense."

"You left the time machine in rather a hurry," he said accusingly, looking rather like a thwarted schoolboy.

"Well?" I said. The suspense was unbearable.

"Can I have my watch back?"

Porridge

Cornflakes is a pastiche of BBC1's TV series, *Porridge*, the brilliant comedy by Dick Clement and Ian La Frenais. Having changed certain characteristics of the warders and inmates of Slade Prison, we felt it appropriate to change their names. So we hope that admirers of those fine actors, Ronnie Barker, Brian Wilde, Fulton Mackay, Peter Vaughan and Richard Beckinsale will forgive us for raising the intellectual and cultural levels of the characters they play. How else could they understand the finer points of bridge?

Cockney Rhyming Slang

For the edification of our American friends, and our upper class English readers, it may be necessary to explain that cockneys are Londoners who were born within the sound of Bow Bells. Much of their speech contains rhyming slang. 'Head' becomes 'loaf of bread', commonly shortened to 'loaf'. The examples overleaf may prove useful if you find yourself an unwilling inmate of Flasher's nick. The word 'nick,' meaning prison or police station, is not rhyming slang. Nor is 'porridge' – to do porridge is to do time.

Slang	Translation
Alan Ladd	Mad
Bathroom tap	Crap
Berkley Hunt (Berk)	Obvious
Birdlime (bird)	Time
Brad Pitt (Brad)	Obvious
Brown Bread	Dead
Camel's hump	Trump
Chevy Chase	Face
Clark Gable	Table
Dicky Bird (Dicky)	Word
Flowery Dell	Cell
Francis Drake	Fake
Gene Kelly	Belly
Half inched	Pinched
Khyber Pass (Khyber)	Posterior
Jam Tarts	Hearts
Little Bo Peep	Sleep
Loaf of Bread (Loaf)	Head
Michael Caine	Brain
Mince Pies	Eyes
Moby Dick	Trick
North and South	Mouth
Oliver Twist	Wrist
Plum Duff	Ruff
Pork Pies (Porkies)	Lies
Rookery Nook	Crook
Sea Breeze	Squeeze
Strawberry Jam	Slam
Tea Leaf	Thief
Tit for Tat (Tit for)	Hat
Uncle Dick	Sick
Upstairs Maids	Spades
Weeping Willow	Pillow

Cornflakes

If you are honest (or lucky) enough never to have done time, you probably think that the average prison is run by the Governor, aided and abetted by that fine body of men known to us cons as "screws". If, like yours truly, you've done more bird than the Count of Monte Cristo, you'll know that the proverbial big stick is wielded by big-time villains like Larry Grouch.

I'm not denying that the Governor has a certain amount of clout. He can remove pay or privileges. But such hardships are fleabites compared with the removal of such useful accessories as kneecaps or front teeth.

That is why, when summoned by the Governor, you amble cheerfully to his office, praying for the erotic sight of his secretary bending over the bottom drawer of her filing cabinet. When Grouchy sends for you, you do not amble, you frigging well gallop, praying that your return journey won't be handicapped by the absence of a few toenails.

So you can imagine my feelings as I stood panting outside his cell door, waiting for my pulse rate to drop to the low hundreds.

"Come in," rasped Grouchy. "It's not locked."

His flowery dell was the height of luxury, as you'll know if you saw its picture in *House and Garden*. Its sole occupant was a thick-set felon with the pasty complexion of the long-server and the mean eyes of the born extortionist. He was reclining on a pink chaise-longue, which went well with his red smoking jacket and his Financial Times. As his right forefinger slid expertly down the Footsie Index, his left pointed to the Regency coffee table, drawing attention to a jug of drinking chocolate and the Cartier watch on his Oliver Twist.

"Help yourself," he offered.

"No, thanks. I'm quite happy with my Timex."

"Very droll, Flasher," he said, baring his gold-filled molars at my shaft of wit.

Don't let my nickname fool you – I ain't in the habit of opening my mac to give biology lessons to defenceless females on Clapham Common. It is a tribute to my legendary speed when pursuing my chosen profession, opening small to medium-sized safes.

I did some quick thinking while sipping Grouchy's chocolate, which was grade-one Belgian. Far from being dischuffed with me, the evil sod wanted a favour. And it must be a big one, or I'd have been lucky to get grade-one dog's droppings.

"How's business?" I asked, playing it cool.

"Don't ask."

"Shares down?"

"Way up." He tossed aside his FT with a yawn.

"Trouble with your prison concessions? Snout? Booze? Hash?"

"Sewn up tighter than a duck's bum," he complained.

"What about Benny Duff?" I probed, referring to his much hated rival. "Has he been giving you bother?"

"Don't make me laugh, Flasher. It's true that I let Duffy pick up a few crumbs from my table. But without a spot of competition, I might find myself in trouble with the Monopolies Commission."

"Things are going well then, Grouchy."

"Too naffing well. It's no joke being the man who has everything."

"Have you tried penicillin?"

"What I'm looking for," he said, ignoring my sally, "is novelty, a fresh challenge, new horizons."

"You could transfer to a bigger nick," I suggested hopefully.

"Not worth the hassle. I'm due for release in two months."

"You'll be sadly missed," I lied, offering silent thanks to the patron saint of convicts, St. Incarceratus.

"Have you heard about the bridge that C Wing are organising?"

"No, Grouchy. But it'll make a change from those naffing tunnels." Then I twigged. "Oh, you mean the card game."

In case you thought that us recidivists can barely cope with the complexities of noughts and crosses, let me tell you that things have changed since Maggie Thatcher invented upward mobility. Our nick can boast a bent judge, four assorted God-botherers, more accountants than they can count, and a poet working on a sequel to the Ballad of Reading Gaol. We also have a bloke who won the Gold Cup, and another who nicked it.

"Do you recall the inter-wing boxing?" Grouchy asked me.

"I'll never forget it," I said. "The thrill of watching favourite after favourite hit the canvas in round one. The warm glow of knowing you'd bet against all eight of them."

"Well C Wing have challenged The Rest to a 24 board team-of-four match."

"I'm afraid, Grouchy, that this news item, thrilling though it is, seeems to have escaped my notice. You'll never get people to bet on bridge."

"At the right odds I could get people to bet Harold won the Battle of Hastings, Flasher. Due to the Governor's crackpot ideas of intellectual segregation, you can't get into C Wing unless you're a Ph-frigging-D, the Chairman of MENSA or a Mastermind finalist. In any competition involving brains, they'd be an automatic 33-1 on. This," he said, handing me a sheet of paper, "is from one of C Wing's weekly news letters. Cast your mince pies over the bridge deal."

Trying not to look as bored as a eunuch at a twelve-day orgy, I focussed my optics on a right load of bathroom tap.

A Revealing Double

♠ A10843
♡ A92
◇ AK2
♣ Q2

♠ 92
♡ Q83
◇ 6
♣ AKJ10765

South	West	North	East
1♣	Dble	Rdbl	1◇
2♣	Pass	6♣	All Pass

West leads the ◇Q.

*If spades are three-three, there is an easy route to thirteen tricks,
but West's double marks him with the ♡K and quite probably four
spades. To cater for this, declarer should play a small heart at trick
two and insert the eight. This rectifies the count for a squeeze
against West.*

*West will probably exit with a diamond, South discarding a
spade. The ♠A and a spade ruff are followed by the ♣K and
another spade ruff. Now when spades fail to break, South runs his
trumps and West is squeezed.*

*Of course, if East has the ♡J10, he will split his honours at trick
two. Declarer should let him hold the trick, as he cannot continue
the suit profitably. Obviously the squeeze against West develops as
before. The full deal is:*

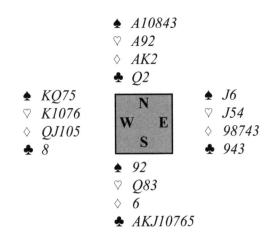

	♠ A10843	
	♡ A92	
	◇ AK2	
	♣ Q2	
♠ KQ75		♠ J6
♡ K1076		♡ J54
◇ QJ105		◇ 98743
♣ 8		♣ 943
	♠ 92	
	♡ Q83	
	◇ 6	
	♣ AKJ10765	

*With this distribution, an inspired East would put in the ♡J at trick
two. Believing he holds the ♡10, declarer will duck and go one
down. However, very few defenders would find this play at the
table.*

"Well?" asked Grouchy, when I had recovered from the excitement.
     "It's all Greek to me," I said.
     "But it gets worse, Flasher. That little article attracted more hate
mail than the naffing Poll Tax. I had it summarised by my contact
at the English Bridge Union. Have a gander at this:"

1.   *Half the initiates of C Wing insist that the ♡J at trick two is a no-cost automatic play, which they would easily find at the table.*

2.   *They point out that declarer should adopt the superior line of ducking a spade at trick two. Now East is helpless.*

"My EBU contact," Grouchy went on, "remarks that he is gobsmacked by C Wing's expertise. He concludes that if he could find a way of depriving his English bridge stars of sex, drink, late nights and rich food, we would have a team of world-beaters."

"In that case, Grouchy," I said, "I would think 33-1 on is too generous."

"Exactly, so I shall be offering 6-4 against."

"I wasn't aware that charity was one of your bad habits. Wasn't it you that said that evil was the root of all money?"

"And that's where you come in, old son. The match will take place four weeks from today. And you, Flasher, are going to fix it."

"Me, Grouchy? Oh, no. My bridge days ended yonks ago. The last straw was when the PBU made me replace my finger signals with a load of poxy conventions."

"I'm counting on you, Flasher. In this nick there are three, maybe four rookery nooks with your diabolical instinct for larceny. But none of them has quite your distaste for torture."

He waved at a pile of bridge books nestling between his Louis-Quinze desk and his state-of-the-art internet.

"I anticipated your state of pig-ignorance," he said, "I shall expect you back here the day after tomorrow. With a cunning plan. So off you go, Flasher. My man Crusher will give you a hand."

The sight of the awesome Crusher Kelly dogging my footsteps with a bundle of books clutched to his 54-inch chest caused many a raised eyebrow. But nobody dared to ask questions, in case they ended up like No Nose Nolan. But when I got back to my flowery dell, my cell mate, Bodger, was full of them.

It is a crying shame that a nice youngster like Denny Bodger was forced by an uncaring society to take up petty burglary. With his innocent eyes, his boyish good looks, and his air of helplessness that would have brought out the mother in Lucrezia Borgia, he'd have made a fortune as a con man.

After I'd briefed him about Grouchy's latest scam, he began to flick through the bridge books.

"Pity," he murmured.

"Sorry, Bodger. Next time I'll get Grouchy to slip in a Jackie Collins and the Kinsey Report."

"Flasher, even amongst the sex-starved inhabitants of Her Majesty's prisons, there are those who appreciate a book for other things than its porn content. But it happens I've read this lot."

Then I remembered. Bodger, whose O level in Geography had gone to his head, had been on every course the nick had to offer; from Origami to Oxy-acetylene Welding. For two perishing months he'd kept me awake reciting bidding sequences in his Little Bo Peep. Until suddenly he'd stopped.

"What made you give it up, Denny?" I asked.

"The standard of play, Flasher."

"Too low?" I sneered.

"At first. When clowns like Dopey Driscoll count their points, you can tell how many they've got by reading their lips. So I tried my luck in C Wing. It was humiliating, Flasher. I felt like Gulliver when he moved from Lilliput to Brobdignag."

Now I was dead worried. That snippet of culture supported my theory that, although Denny's IQ was nothing to write home about, at least he had one. This made him the Einstein of our social circle. And if he'd lost his shirt to the eggheads of C Wing, our bunch of Laurel and Hardys would have less chance of beating them than getting the Three Tenors to sing at our Christmas concert.

"But I told you about it at the time," Bodger was complaining. "You weren't listening, were you?"

"In those days, young Denny, renewing my acquaintance with a poxy card game was not a matter of life and death."

"It is now, Flash."

"So tell me, what exactly is a twenty-four board team-of-four match when it's at home?"

Denny promptly began to wax lyrical on the dubious joys of competitive bridge. My face fell when he told me those cheating Bar Stewards in C Wing used screens. But I perked up when he explained duplicate boards. And the idea of pre-dealt hands sent a tingle up my felonious spine. If my instinct for larceny was at its diabolical best, we had the enemy by the short and curlies.

Two weeks later my good friend Mr Barrow wandered gingerly into our recreation area, wearing his usual expression of a basset hound who's just discovered he is ten miles from the nearest tree. The Barrow is one of those screws who believe that, if you feed prisoners on the milk of human kindness, they will repay you with a lifetime of honest work. There is a scientific term for someone who believes this theory. Berk.

He arrived at the bridge table just in time to watch Dopey Driscol in an iffy four spades. An expert will spot the best line in five seconds flat, but bear in mind that on a good morning it takes Dopey ten minutes to work out which shoe goes on which foot.

Game All. Dealer West.

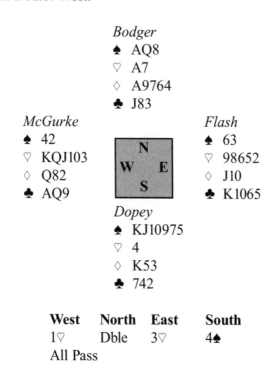

```
                   Bodger
                   ♠  AQ8
                   ♡  A7
                   ◊  A9764
                   ♣  J83
   McGurke                          Flash
   ♠  42            ┌─────────┐     ♠  63
   ♡  KQJ103        │    N    │     ♡  98652
   ◊  Q82          W│         │E    ◊  J10
   ♣  AQ9           │    S    │     ♣  K1065
                   └─────────┘
                   Dopey
                   ♠  KJ10975
                   ♡  4
                   ◊  K53
                   ♣  742
```

West	North	East	South
1♡	Dble	3♡	4♠
All Pass			

Sweat poured from the corrugated Driscoll brow as he gazed at the ♡K lead, but he surprised Mr Barrow by calling for dummy's ♡7. Now LHO was Jocko McGurke, the Glasgow axe murderer, not a man you'd expect to be paralysed with indecision. But he just sat there as if unaware that he was still on lead.

"Chop, chop!" I said, forgetting who I was talking to, but he let me off with a black look and continued with the queen of jam tarts. Gurgling childishly, Dopey threw a diamond on the ♡A. Then he cashed the ◇AK and plum duffed a third round, setting up the diamonds for club discards.

Mr Barrow opened the post mortem with an apologetic cough. "That was well played, Driscoll. It was very courageous to duck the first trick."

"We don't call him Daring Dopey for nothing," Bodger intervened. "But it was obvious to a man of his perspicatiousness that Jocko couldn't have the two top clubs, or he would have led one, wouldn't he?"

"Ah, yes. So he banked on a passive defence."

"Right," said Bodger, cutting short Dopey's sub-human grunt.

"It's very gratifying, the progress you've made," said Mr B. "Only a few days ago, I heard Driscoll open the bidding with One Clover. It speaks volumes for your training, Bodger. I suppose you owe it to that fortnight's course on instructional techniques."

"True," I chimed in. "But he owes even more to that month's course on brain surgery."

As the puzzled screw shuffled off, I decided to give Driscoll a positive stroke. "Well done, Dopey," I said. "That's only the twelfth time we've played that hand, and you've already got it right."

In case you haven't sussed the subtleties of our selection strategy, I should explain that with Dopey in the team, nobody, but nobody, would spoil Grouchy's clean sheet by betting on us. Bodger's innocent face would be a great asset in removing suspicion when certain nefarious deeds were perpetrated. McGurke's talent for going down in 3NT with eleven on top was a slight handicap, but at least we could be sure that nobody would dare to double him.

I owed my own place to the kind heart of Larry Grouch. He wanted me to be there at the finish, so that if everything went pear-shaped, the awesome Crusher could grab me by the extremities before I had time to cut my throat.

Yet despite the prospect of losing my manhood, I was confident that after another dozen dry runs, Dopey would make four spades without breaking sweat. While at the other table Bodger and I would get it two off by finding the evil club switch at trick two.

Young Bodger was rightly proud of this deal, but I had a feeling in my water that we needed some professional help, and that was only available in C Wing, where honour amongst thieves was a religion. There was no way any one of them would rat on his mates for four ounces of snout. We'd have to come up with half a pound.

For eight ounces of Golden Virginia and a large tin of pineapple chunks, we acquired the services of – to use one of his many aliases – the Honourable Freddie Burlington-Smythe, Onfred for short. His most notable swindles were in the lucrative field of high-stake gambling. The perfect mole.

"All C Wing's matches are played in conditions of maximum security," he told us, during a candlestine visit to our cell.

"Very wise," I said. "There's a rumour that one or two of our fellow inmates are potential criminals."

He looked at me as if I was something unpleasant he'd found on the sole of his shoe. "The English Bridge Union will despatch a printout of twenty-four deals," he continued. It will immediately be taken by a warder to the Governor's secretary, who will make up the hands and place them in the boards, which she will put in the prison safe. Five minutes before the match begins, they will be delivered to the recreation room by two random warders."

"Why random?" asked the naive Bodger.

"Since half the screws are on Grouchy's payroll, I should have thought that was obvious," sniffed Onfred, as he examined his beautifully manicured fingernails. "So now, Flasher, I am sure that, as the prison's Napoleon of crime, you have sufficient data to determine your *modus operandi* for the substitution."

"Oh, absolutely," I said. "Er, what exactly does this printout look like?"

"I'm glad you asked," he smiled, producing a sheet of paper. "This is from the final of our last teams-of-four championship. I kept it as a memento of my victory."

"Thanks, Onfred. Very useful. I'll give it to our resident forger."

"You won't need a forger, Flasher. You'll need Grouchy's computer. But do make sure you use the correct font."

"Oh, naturally, Onfred, naturally."

"Now let's discuss our strategy for selecting the deals. I've brought some examples."

"Go ahead, Onfred," I said. "We're a captive audience."

Love All. Dealer South.

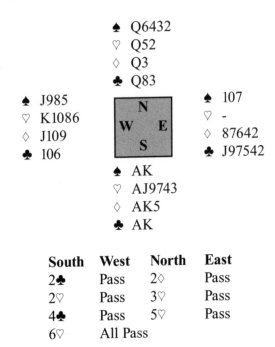

	♠ Q6432	
	♡ Q52	
	◇ Q3	
	♣ Q83	
♠ J985		♠ 107
♡ K1086		♡ -
◇ J109		◇ 87642
♣ 106		♣ J97542
	♠ AK	
	♡ AJ9743	
	◇ AK5	
	♣ AK	

South	West	North	East
2♣	Pass	2◇	Pass
2♡	Pass	3♡	Pass
4♣	Pass	5♡	Pass
6♡	All Pass		

"The ◇J is led," said Onfred. "I've shown you the complete layout, because West's trump holding is exactly what a cautious expert would cater for. Seeing all four hands, Bodger, how would you proceed?"

While Denny went into the think tank, I decided to show Onfred I was by no means the mug he took me for. "He'd take in dummy," I said.

"Actually he should take in hand, Flasher. But congratulations for winning the second prize."

"Well," Bodger took over, "having won *in hand*, I suppose I should lead a heart towards dummy's queen."

"Correct, dear boy. It wins and you discover the bad break. But, being adept at trump reduction, you greet it with a contemptuous curl of the lip. After cashing the black ace-kings, you play a diamond to the queen and ruff a spade. Now you are ready to win a round of applause from these kibitzers who have never seen a grand coup before, by ruffing your ◇A in dummy. Another spade ruff sets the scene for the three-card ending in which you will endplay the unfortunate West."

"Well played, Bodger," I said. "I never knew you had it in you. But I'm wondering whether the opposition will credit you with the nous to come up with that grand whatsit."

"He won't," announced Onfred. "He will make the palooka play of winning the opening lead in dummy, then he will take the trump finesse and make an overtrick. Because, my friends, this will be the actual deal:"

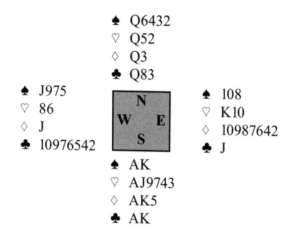

```
                    ♠ Q6432
                    ♡ Q52
                    ◇ Q3
                    ♣ Q83
  ♠ J975          ┌─────────┐      ♠ 108
  ♡ 86            │    N    │      ♡ K10
  ◇ J             │  W   E  │      ◇ 10987642
  ♣ 10976542      │    S    │      ♣ J
                  └─────────┘
                    ♠ AK
                    ♡ AJ9743
                    ◇ AK5
                    ♣ AK
```

"When East wins with the ♡K, he will give his partner a diamond ruff. Damned bad luck for our expert South, what?"

"It occurs to me, Onfred," I said, "that apart from the half pound of shag and the pineapple chunks, you have another motive for helping us to duff up C Wing. Be honest; I won't shop you to the Con Man's Union."

"I don't approve of their team," he said.

"Don't tell me that you're not in it!"

"The selectors decided to blood some youngsters. Their average age is forty-five."

"It's a flippin' scandal," said Bodger.

"Thank you, dear boy. But I intend to exact every last ounce of revenge. The first twelve boards will be so average that, if both teams were competent, there would be no significant swings."

"But," I objected, "in describing our lot, competent would not be the word that springs to mind."

"Quite. Even foolproof contracts might not survive the inspired lunacy of Driscoll and McGurke. But we can offset those losses by arranging for you and Denny to keep your opponents out of game by hair-raising overcalls. In view of your tendency to live dangerously, this will arouse no suspicion. By half time we should restrict C Wing's juvenile quartet to a slight lead."

"How slight?"

"Twenty imps at the most."

"Twenty! Did I hear you say twenty?"

"Calm down, Flasher. In the second half ..."

"Onfred, when Grouchy hears we're twenty imps adrift, there will be no bleedin' second half. He'll call off all bets on account of his entire team being brown bread."

"Flasher, you may be an authority on the cruder forms of theft, but when it comes to the big con, your ignorance is staggering. You always begin by letting the mark win a little."

"Soften him up, like," said Bodger.

"Precisely. Then in the second half, C Wing will find that Lady Luck is a fickle mistress. Expert lines will fail where palooka lines succeed. You will find bizarre defences that prove to be brilliancies in disguise."

"Well, why can't we do all that in the first half?"

"Let me fill some of the holes in your education," he sighed, producing another hand:

Game All. Dealer South.

♠ J874
♡ 6
♢ AK9753
♣ 84

♠ A963
♡ A3
♢ Q642
♣ KQ3

West	North	East	South
			1♠
4♡	4♠	Dble	All Pass

"The contract is Four Spades, doubled by East, and you, Flasher, are South. After the lead of the ♡K, I invite you to do your worst."

"A piece of cake," I said, after no more than two minutes of high quality thought. "I win the trick and bash out two rounds of trumps."

"I said you loved living dangerously," nodded Onfred. "But suppose this was the full hand:"

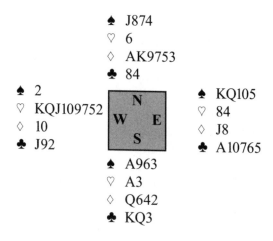

```
              ♠ J874
              ♡ 6
              ◊ AK9753
              ♣ 84
♠ 2                        ♠ KQ105
♡ KQJ109752               ♡ 84
◊ 10                       ◊ J8
♣ J92                      ♣ A10765
              ♠ A963
              ♡ A3
              ◊ Q642
              ♣ KQ3
```

"Now you will have bashed your way to a 2300 penalty. Even a semi-expert would begin by playing a low spade from hand. Then he would pick up the suit for two losers."

"So I'll play it like a semi-expert."

"No. You'll handle trumps like a semi-idiot. Because on the big day, this will be the full distribution:"

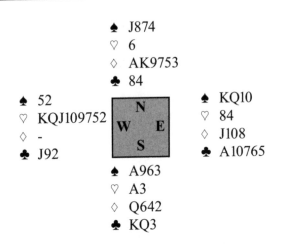

"You will observe that when East takes the first round of trumps and gives his partner a diamond ruff, the expert line fails. Whereas you will bash your way to victory."

"So I was right all the time then," I muttered.

"I have shown you two deals with a similar theme. Now if we included them in the first half, can you imagine what would happen when they scored up at half time?"

"They'd smell a rat," said Bodger.

"And start taking mug's lines on tricky contracts," said Onfred.

"So we'll save our more ingenious deals for the second half. And we'll vary our tactics."

We had three plans for switching the printouts. Plan A was to trip up the screw on his way from the mail room, causing him to let go of the Governor's post. Then, while helping him to collect his droppings, we would switch the envelopes. This plan was so full of holes that you have probably guessed it was Bodger's.

Plan B was to make the switch as soon as the mail reached the Governor's office. This had slightly fewer holes than plan A, but it was rejected in favour of plan C, based on evidence that in the eighty year history of our beloved hoosegow, nobody had ever done the Governor's safe.

Recently, I had wangled the cushy job of wheeling a book trolley round the nick, and dispensing its contents to those lags who had a taste for reading matter which contained no crime, sex, violence or bad language. Having served all three of my customers, I arrived at the Governor's den on his secretary's day off, and at a time when he was away on some routine duty, such as a round of golf. It took me three seconds to unlock his door and another twelve to open the safe. Having substituted our duplicate boards for the genuine articles, I relocked everything. The whole caper had taken less than a minute.

On my return journey, I winked at the three cons who had been posted to distract any approaching screws, and was about to congratulate myself on a job well done, when I found myself face-to-face with that charmless Caledonian berk, Mr McLeish.

Rating sympathy for incarcerated felons on a scale of 0-10, McLeish, on one of his more benevolent days, scores minus two. And there he stood, barring my path, and casting a gimlet eye on my trolley, with it's four dozen turgid tomes and two dozen green plastic duplicate boards.

"Good afternoon, Mr McLeish," I greeted him. "You're looking very chipper."

"And you, Flasher, are looking very mendacious."

In case this gives you the impression that the hard man of screwdom was educated, I should explain that he had memorised every known word describing chicanery, dishonesty, and the other desirable criminal qualities.

"You're way off your normal beat," he said. "Have you been delivering to the Governor?"

"I was, sir. But he seems to have escaped."

"None of your lip, Flasher. Give me the book that he wanted and I'll make sure that he gets it."

On the outside I'd have known how to deal with situations like that. When a copper stops you in the street and tells you to open a suitcase full of hot jewellery, you hurl the swag in his face and leg it. But in the nick, there's no place to leg it to. So I grabbed the nearest volume and shoved it into McLeish's hot sweaty hand.

He peered suspiciously at the title. "*The Tale of Squirrel Nutkin* by Beatrix Potter," he announced with a nasty grin. "Now I know why you're always putting one over on the Governor. He's in his second childhood. But you're not fooling me, Flasher."

As he examined the duplicate boards, you could almost see the wheels turning in what, in the back streets of Glasgow, probably passed for a Michael Caine.

"Playing cards!" he exclaimed.

"Amazing, Holmes!" I exclaimed back at him.

"I've got you to rights, Flasher. It's all about the bridge match between C Wing and The Rest. And you've nicked these from the Governor's safe. Admit it, you miserable melafactor. You're fixing the match."

"Mr McLeish," I said, realising I was up to my ankles in the Brad Pitt, "what can I say?"

"Don't say anything, Flasher," his hand dipped into his inside pocket and came out clutching a bundle of banknotes. "Just keep your mouth shut and put that lot on The Rest."

I'll say one thing for our team. Like the Dallas Aces, we played in identical uniforms. As Onfred had planned, the match began with four boards that were as flat as Shirley Bassey's top C. Then Dopey Driscoll went down in a game he'd made six times in practice – a classic case of overtraining.

On board six, Bodger made amends by landing this juicy strawberry jam with, I am reliably informed, a combined total of sixteen HCP.

North/South Game. Dealer South.

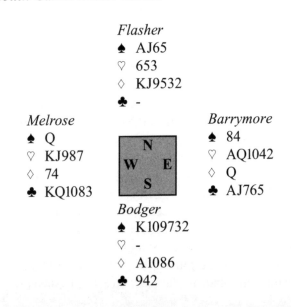

Flasher
- ♠ AJ65
- ♡ 653
- ◇ KJ9532
- ♣ -

Melrose
- ♠ Q
- ♡ KJ987
- ◇ 74
- ♣ KQ1083

Barrymore
- ♠ 84
- ♡ AQ1042
- ◇ Q
- ♣ AJ765

Bodger
- ♠ K109732
- ♡ -
- ◇ A1086
- ♣ 942

South	West	North	East
1♠	2♡	4♣	4♡
5♡	Pass	5♠	Pass
6♢	Pass	7♠	Dble
All Pass			

Seven Spades was a doddle. But we were proud of our auction – not the bids, but the way we agonised over every one of them. Not easy when you know thirteen tricks are on ice.

Melrose, a big-time embezzler with a constipated expression and the physique of an undernourished stick insect, went for his partner's throat.

"You made it childishly easy for them, Lionel," he said. "If you'd bid Six Hearts on the second round they'd never have reached the grand."

"Possibly," agreed Barrymore, a jolly-faced tycoon who, being halfway through a five stretch for bribery and corruption, was a great favourite with the screws.

"Well played, Denny," I said, interrupting another load of grief from Miseryguts Melrose.

"Outstanding," agreed Melrose. "The idea of ruffing a club in dummy was particularly brilliant."

"Now, now, Melrose," I objected. "My partner and me are *imprevious* to sarcasm, but it drives my kibitzer to acts of X-rated violence."

As my kibitzer was the awesome Crusher Kelly, one warning did the trick.

Then came my brilliancy. It was selected by Onfred to demoralise our opponents without arousing their suspicion, because the winning line would only be found by an expert or a novice.

Guess which he said I was.

Game All. Dealer West.

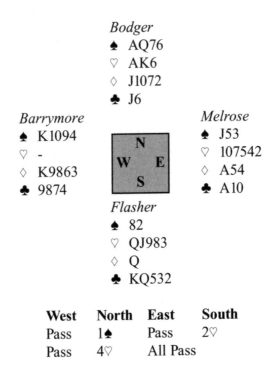

Bodger
- ♠ AQ76
- ♡ AK6
- ◇ J1072
- ♣ J6

Barrymore
- ♠ K1094
- ♡ -
- ◇ K9863
- ♣ 9874

Melrose
- ♠ J53
- ♡ 107542
- ◇ A54
- ♣ A10

Flasher
- ♠ 82
- ♡ QJ983
- ◇ Q
- ♣ KQ532

West	North	East	South
Pass	1♠	Pass	2♡
Pass	4♡	All Pass	

Barrymore led the ♠10. I took the finesse and managed to look relieved when it worked. Then I led dummy's ♣J. Melrose won with the ace and continued upstairs maids. I am told that at this point even a fair to middling player might make the mistake of cashing a top trump. Now his chances wouldn't be worth a sparrow's fart.

According to the Gospel of St Onfred, if trumps were 4-1 and clubs were 4-2 the contract was cold, possibly for an overtrick. So all I needed to worry about was a 5-0 trump break.

Following orders, I crossed to my ♣K and cashed the ♡Q. The obscenity which escaped my lips was a two-way bid. It showed disgust both at the bad break and my own poxy suit-handling.

Of course, as a real bridge player, you will raise your tit for tat to Onfred. If both defenders had followed, I would ruff a club high, cash the ♡A, ruff a spade and make ten or eleven tricks, depending on the heart break.

The layout being what it was, I simply ruffed two clubs high and made my small trumps by ruffing spades.

"You nearly cocked that one up, Flasher, leading your trump queen," commented Bodger, right on cue.

"I know, Denny," I replied, shaking my head in shame and sorrow. "I must have been Alan Ladd."

"Well, insanity seems to suit you," moaned Melrose. "If you tackle the trumps in the normal way, you go down."

He launched into a speech that went ten feet over my loaf.

"Quite right," agreed Barrymore. "Congratulations, Flasher. You played like an expert of the second rank."

"Oh?" said Melrose. "And what would those in the first rank have done?"

"I might concede a diamond at trick two," said Barrymore.

His explanation went twenty feet over my head. This is one of the reasons why I gave up bridge. When a pool player misses, you don't hear a bunch of clever dicks rabbiting about whether he should have put more Irish on the shot, more chalk on his cue or more lead in his pencil.

But one thing pleased me. If Barrymore's line was superior, that was one in the eye for big-headed Onfred. I was less chuffed later, when I learned that our opponents had crossed-ruffed their way to ten tricks after following Barrymore's suggested line.

And worse was to come. Two boards later, Melrose made a laydown four spades. In the other room, Jocko McGurke, who had been instructed to spread his hand, showed off his new found skill by playing them out. He was doing quite well till he pulled a wrong card. The aggro when he tried to take it back was brought to a halt by a few words of condolence from his LHO (a defrocked bishop), and a violent crack on the nut from a thoughtful screw.

Jocko must have enjoyed the experience, because on the next hand he revoked twice.

Scoring up at half time was not one of the highlights of my week. The bad news was that Jocko had put all his scores in the minus column. The good news was that only eight of them were wrong. Dopey had expressed his contempt for large numbers by writing "1 off," "2 off" or "maid". So we borrowed the defrocked bishop's card and discovered we were eighteen imps down.

I tried to catch Onfred's eye, but he was jawing away to Mr Barrow. All of a sudden my jam tart was in my north and south.

Two weeks ago, the Barrow had watched Dopey Driscoll make that Four Spades by ducking the lead. And he was about to see me and Bodger defeat the same contract by playing three rounds of clubs. Board thirteen was a disaster waiting to happen!

My Michael Caine went into top gear. Barrow may have been less streetwise than Red Riding Hood, but he wasn't a complete mug. So I played on his other fatal weakness – a kind heart.

"Mr Barrow," I gasped, oozing agony from every pore. "You wouldn't have a couple of Panadols on you, would you?"

"Why, Flasher? Are you ill?"

"I've an agonising pain in my Gene Kelly."

"Would aspirins do?"

"Daren't touch 'em, Mr Barrow. Not with my bleeding ulcer. The trouble is the match is about to restart and I daren't keep C Wing waiting. If I'm late back they'll dock us five imps a minute."

"Late back from what, Flasher?"

"From my cell. That's where my Panadols are. Under my weeping willow, if I remember rightly."

"Are you asking me to fetch a banned substance?"

"What a kind suggestion, Mr Barrow. It'll save my life."

He went off like a lamb. I calculated that it would take him a minute and a half each way, plus another three minutes to discover that the nearest thing in my flowery dell to a Panadol was a Rowntree's fruit pastille I'd been saving for Bodger's birthday.

Board thirteen went like a dream. The bishop found the duck, and rolled his eyes heavenwards when Bodger found the killing club switch. But divine help was not forthcoming. The cards were back in the board when the Barrow returned, looking miffed.

"There were no Panadols in your cell, Flasher," he said. "Will this Rowntree's fruit pastille be of any use?"

"Sorry, Mr B. Someone must have half inched the Panadols, but knowing you, you'll soon cut the list of suspects down to six hundred."

Two partscores followed. Partscores are harder to predict than games and slams, so we expected to lose a little. But were we downhearted? Too bloody right we were! According to Onfred, four of the remaining boards were sure swings in our favour. But we'd already seen what butchery our other pair was capable of, and they hadn't even warmed up yet.

I'm told that the next hand will be familiar to most masters, but keep your hair on – there is a sting in the tail. By the way, I have been advised to remind you that all hands have been rotated for convenience.

Love All. Dealer South.

Leonardo Smith
♠ K974
♡ A43
◇ 1076
♣ 763

Bodger
♠ Q1053
♡ Q85
◇ J85
♣ Q102

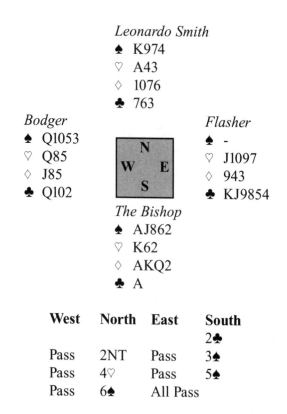

Flasher
♠ -
♡ J1097
◇ 943
♣ KJ9854

The Bishop
♠ AJ862
♡ K62
◇ AKQ2
♣ A

West	North	East	South
			2♣
Pass	2NT	Pass	3♠
Pass	4♡	Pass	5♠
Pass	6♠	All Pass	

Leonardo was not Smithy's real name. It was bestowed on him as a master forger who flogged Francis Drakes of famous paintings to Texas oil barons. Against the upstairs maid strawberry jam, Bodger led the ◇5. The Bishop called for dummy's ◇10 and, when it held the trick, saw that his only problem was limiting his trump tricks to one.

His Grace, who had got away with several hundred cases of illicit nookie before finally being caught with his pants round his ankles, was a dab hand at safety plays. He crossed to his ♣A and led a low spade towards dummy, intending to insert the seven. If

West went in with the ten, he would win with dummy's king, ruff a club and advance the ♠J. Bodger would have no answer to this. Basically, the bishop intended to ruff two clubs in hand and discard a heart on a winning diamond.

Visualising a layout like the above, that was his plan, so how did he go down? Because I lied. This was the actual distribution:

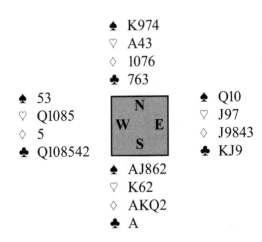

```
                    ♠ K974
                    ♡ A43
                    ◇ 1076
                    ♣ 763
    ♠ 53                          ♠ Q10
    ♡ Q1085          N            ♡ J97
    ◇ 5          W       E        ◇ J9843
    ♣ Q108542        S            ♣ KJ9
                    ♠ AJ862
                    ♡ K62
                    ◇ AKQ2
                    ♣ A
```

On the opening lead, when dummy's ◇10 was played, I found the nutty looking play of the ◇3. Now the bishop couldn't possibly place my partner with a singleton. So when I came in with the ♠10, I returned a diamond to give Denny a plum duff.

"Amazing," said the Bishop. "How on earth did you find that play of a low diamond?"

"I didn't realise I had the jack," I lied. "I had it mixed up with my jam tarts."

"But you had the jack of hearts," he said. "Surely you would have noticed the two red knaves in such close proximity."

"I did, after I'd played the low diamond. I was going to ask if I could take it back, but because of your holy presence I had a sudden attack of ethics."

"Don't worry, Flasher," said Leonardo. "I'm sure my partner will absolve you."

At that moment, one of Grouchy's errand boys arrived, a small-time tea leaf called Creepy Catchpole. He was looking as innocent as a fox in a hen roost, and clutching an envelope.

"Excuse me," he said. "But I've got a note for Flasher."

"I'm sorry, Catchpole, but there must be no communication with the players during the match. It's against the rules," said the Bishop.

"But it's only ..."

"Sorry, Creepy," said Leonardo. "You'll just have to wait. Mr Barrow is the official referee. He'll confirm it."

"Will I?" asked Mr B, with that look of childish bewilderment we knew and loved. "Well, if you say it's against the rules I suppose I must."

Creepy left, looking a trifle Uncle Dick, and after a supposedly flat board, this deal arrived. And I'll begin by confirming that once again I am telling porkies. Declarer thought that the defenders' cards were those in the following diagram.

East/West Game. Dealer South.

Leonardo Smith
- ♠ K976
- ♡ 8
- ◊ Q109865
- ♣ A3

Bodger
- ♠ Q532
- ♡ Q1076
- ◊ A
- ♣ J1082

```
      N
   W     E
      S
```

Flasher
- ♠ 108
- ♡ J9542
- ◊ K7
- ♣ KQ74

The Bishop
- ♠ AJ4
- ♡ AK3
- ◊ J432
- ♣ 965

South	West	North	East
1◊	Pass	1♠	Pass
1NT	Pass	3◊	Pass
4♠	Pass	5◊	All Pass

I am reliably informed that the bidding was a bit naff, but the final contract was kosher. Bodger led the ♣J, won in dummy. Declarer pitched a club on a top heart and ruffed a club. Then he led dummy's ◊Q, won by Bodger's ace. Young Denny exited with a third heart, which was ruffed on the Clark Gable. Now the Bishop played a spade to the *ace* and ruffed his remaining club before exiting with a diamond. As you can see, East would have been up a well-known creek without a paddle. He could give a ruff and discard, or lead the ♠10. The Bishop would cover with the ♠J and kiss goodbye to his spade loser.

But here is the real layout:

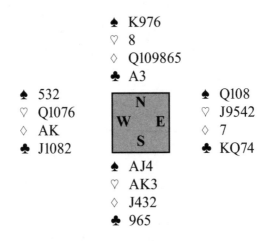

```
              ♠ K976
              ♡ 8
              ◊ Q109865
              ♣ A3
♠ 532                        ♠ Q108
♡ Q1076          N           ♡ J9542
◊ AK         W       E       ◊ 7
♣ J1082          S           ♣ KQ74
              ♠ AJ4
              ♡ AK3
              ◊ J432
              ♣ 965
```

When Bodger's ◊K appeared, the Bishop's ghast was well and truly flabbered. "I can't believe it!" he said. "Only a fool or a genius would have refrained from cashing two top trumps at the first opportunity."

"True," grinned Leonardo. "Which are you, young Bodger?"

"The jury's still out," I informed him.

It was at this point that Grouchy's second messenger arrived, one Denny the Dip, a tragic victim of the cashless society. Unlike Creepy, he came in without the fanfare of trumpets, edged casually past my chair and the next thing I knew an envelope appeared on my lap. As far as I could see, nobody else spotted this, possibly because they were too busy putting their hands in their pockets to protect their valuables.

After two boards which were as flat as Twiggy's chest, this one turned up:

Love All. Dealer South.

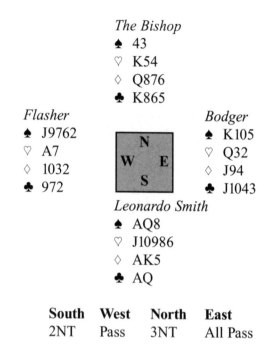

The Bishop
- ♠ 43
- ♡ K54
- ◇ Q876
- ♣ K865

Flasher
- ♠ J9762
- ♡ A7
- ◇ 1032
- ♣ 972

Bodger
- ♠ K105
- ♡ Q32
- ◇ J94
- ♣ J1043

Leonardo Smith
- ♠ AQ8
- ♡ J10986
- ◇ AK5
- ♣ AQ

South	West	North	East
2NT	Pass	3NT	All Pass

I led the ♠6, and Denny Bodger put up his king, which held. Leonardo took the second round, and I followed with the ♠2. Then declarer ran the ♡J. Denny won and cleared spades. Now Leonardo was on a guess. Should he play for diamonds to break 3-3 or for the ♡A to be on his right? I gather that continuing jam tarts is the percentage play, and Onfred expected a decent declarer to take it and go down. But an expert like Leonardo, he said, would look for an extra edge.

He was right. Leonardo spotted it. After winning the second spade, he cashed the ♣AQ and continued with the ◇K. We were very likely to signal length, as it looked as if declarer was trying to force an entry to dummy.

Of course we had been well briefed by our resident con man. So Denny produced his ◇9 and I chipped in with my ◇3.

Leonardo studied our cards for half a minute. Then he studied our Chevy Chases for the other half. Then he grinned like a Cheshire cat. He continued with the ◇A and a small diamond. Against the odds he'd landed his nine Moby Dicks.

Our false carding had been as much use as a eunuch's jock strap.

By now we were waiting for boards, so I had a chance to open my envelope without being clocked. There was a note inside. It said. "Throw the match."

It wasn't signed. Grouchy never signed anything. But the coat of arms at the top of the page was his, and the visits of Creepy and Denny confirmed it. Mine was not to reason why – I had to throw the match. And there were only two boards left.

On the first I was in Three No Trumps with eleven on top if two finesses worked, and I knew they would. By using all my skill, I managed to lose four tricks, but that was the best I could do.

By a cruel twist of fate, I could do sweet F.A. to help chuck the last hand. It all depended on Bodger. I couldn't slip Grouchy's note to him, because at least ten pairs of mince pies were watching me. I thought of praying, but the Bishop was declarer and God obviously had it in for him.

Love All. Dealer South.

```
                    ♠ 74
                    ♡ Q32
                    ◊ KQ982
                    ♣ 853
   ♠ Q10853                        ♠ J9
   ♡ 1084           N              ♡ J9765
   ◊ 7653        W     E           ◊ AJ10
   ♣ Q             S               ♣ 974
                    ♠ AK62
                    ♡ AK
                    ◊ 4
                    ♣ AKJ1062
```

South	West	North	East
2♣	Pass	2◊	Pass
3♣	Pass	3◊	Pass
3♠	Pass	4♣	Pass
4♡	Pass	4♠	Pass
6♣	All Pass		

I warn you once again I have given Denny and me the cards His Grace thought we had. You'll soon see why. By now my mild dislike of Onfred had been replaced by violent hatred. I was a nervous wreck. If I'd fixed the hands myself, Denny and I would have led the life of Riley, making ten percent games and slams and beating cast-iron contracts with mad opening leads. But Onfred was too clever by half. The man took more risks than Evil Knievel. I should have remembered what he was inside for – flogging a phoney gold mine to the Chief Constable.

Bodger led a spade. The Bishop won and cashed the ♣A, dropping Denny's bare queen. Then he froze. I knew why, of course. The stage was set for another Onfred Spectacular. Declarer's problem is to find an entry to dummy's red queens. The Bishop knew how to do it, but the memory of previous cock-ups was giving him the yips.

The trick is to cash the major suit ace-kings. Then a diamond to the king fixes East. If I turn up with a third spade, declarer gets home by ruffing the third round. Any red card gives the lead to dummy. And if I play trumps, dummy's ♣8 provides the entry. Unless ...

But you've seen the catch, haven't you?

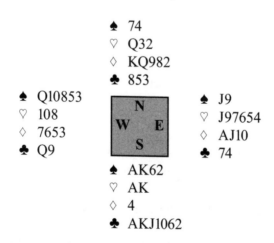

```
              ♠ 74
              ♡ Q32
              ◇ KQ982
              ♣ 853
♠ Q10853                      ♠ J9
♡ 108            N            ♡ J97654
◇ 7653      W       E         ◇ AJ10
♣ Q9            S            ♣ 74
              ♠ AK62
              ♡ AK
              ◇ 4
              ♣ AKJ1062
```

You were right. The artful Bodger had dropped the queen from Q9 doubleton. Now when I led a trump, he would make an unexpected Moby Dick with the ♣9.

A furtive glance told me the possibility of a swindle had

occurred to declarer. But he couldn't be sure, so I decided to give the old buffer a helpful nudge. I caught Denny's eye and gave him a crafty wink, accompanied by a diabolical leer. And Denny's response was perfect. His face went as red as Hiawatha's Khyber Pass after a week in the saddle.

From these subtle hints of villainy and guilt the Bishop couldn't help concluding that dirty work was afoot, so he simply led a diamond to the king, won my spade return, drew another round of trumps and claimed.

"Bless you, Bishop," I breathed a sigh of relief. "You played that like Omar Khayam. How you saw through my partner's scam, I'll never know. You must have led a very wicked life."

I couldn't wait to score up. I knew our teammates hadn't let us down and I was right. They had bid out of turn, played out of turn and dropped more points than an Olympic gymnast landing on his nut. We'd lost by more than twenty imps.

Young Bodger's face was as long as a life sentence, but there was no time for explanations. I was on my way to pay my respects to Larry Grouch. But round the first corner I was waylaid by a vicious looking Mr McLeish, who was breathing fire and spitting haggis.

"You've done me, Flasher," he said. "I wagered a large sum on your team because you told me you'd fixed the match."

"No, I didn't, Mr McLeish. You jumped to conclusions. You instructed me to bet your bundle against C Wing and before I could say a dicky bird you'd made off as fast as your guilty conscience could carry you. If you'll forgive me for saying so, sir, it's a clear case of *honny soir key mally ponce*[1]."

I knew I was saying goodbye to the book trolley and hello to scrubbing the latrines, but it was worth it.

Crusher was standing guard outside the dreaded cell, his lips compressed in a straight line. As this was the nearest he ever got to a beam of delight, I marched into Grouchy's presence with a confident swagger.

"You did it, old son," he said. "I'm glad you got my note in time."

---

[1] *Honi soit qui mal y pense.* (Evil be to him who evil thinks.)

"I got it, I acted on it, but I didn't naffing well understand it, Grouchy. Why did you want me to throw the match?"

"Benny Duff," he said. "Just before half time, the crafty git paid me a visit and bet a bundle on you. I couldn't lose face by refusing the bet, could I? So I decided to teach him a lesson."

"But how did he find out about the fix?" I asked.

"My enquiries indicate that he received a tip from a certain party. At this very moment my associates are having a word in his shell-like. He's called Burlington-Smythe."

"You mean Onfred. His name's Freddie."

He glanced at his Cartier. "No," he said. "It's just been changed to Gummy."

"But you must have ended up with a losing book," I said.

"It was worth it to score off Benny," he said. "And it's all down to you, Flasher. So you'd better go off and celebrate. And there'll be something for you in your Christmas stocking."

The world didn't seem such a bad place as I ambled back to my cell. I was well in with the almighty Grouchy, I'd put one over on McLeish. Cleaning bogs wasn't my idea of a career step, but within a week I should corner the toilet roll market. And getting onto Grouchy's Christmas list was the nick's equivalent of being mentioned in the New Year Honours List.

I was halfway back to my cell before it dawned on me that Grouchy was due out in six weeks. And it was only April.

The Fatal Five

As I drove towards Poirot's headquarters, I pictured the little man with the egg-shaped head, green eyes and that preposterous waxed moustache. I imagined his delight on beholding me and his excitement when I showed him the contents of the envelope I carried in my breast pocket.

I knew that the great Hercule Poirot was sure to be at home. No longer did his investigations draw him to the four corners of the world. Even his wealthiest and most distinguished clients were compelled to bring their problems to his well-protected chambers, and wait while he solved them from the comfort of his armchair.

After Security had examined my bona fides, I raced up the stairs one at a time and knocked on Poirot's door.

"*Entrez*," cried the familiar voice. "*Mon ami*, Hastings!" it continued excitedly as I entered the room, and I marvelled, not for the first time, that a man who had mastered phrases such as 'the evidence of the blood stains is incontrovertible', could not learn the English for '*mon ami*'.

"How are you, Poirot?" I enquired fluently.

"Hastings," said Poirot. "My struggle against the Fatal Five approaches its climax. Within days either I will have the evidence which will enable Scotland Yard to smash their evil empire, or I, Hercule Poirot, will perish."

I smiled inwardly at Poirot's obsession with an imaginary association of master criminals bent on the destruction of civilisation as we know it. His favourite delusion was that one of their members, the Liquidator, was a master of disguise, able to impersonate characters of any age, gender or nationality while executing death sentences on their enemies.

"My dear Poirot," I soothed him, "compared with such an undertaking, the puzzle I have brought you seems trivial. It is a bridge deal, a small slam which was made by a person whose identity I do not know, but who I am assured is a murderer whose ruthlessness and ingenuity defies belief."

Before he could resist, I had torn open my envelope and thrust before him this irresistible deal:

East/West Game. Dealer East.

♠ A5
♡ KQ87
◇ KJ754
♣ K3

♠ 63
♡ A432
◇ AQ1096
♣ A4

South	West	North	East
			3♣
3◇	4♠	4NT	Pass
5♠	Pass	6◇	All Pass

"West leads the ♠K," I informed Poirot, as he gazed at the tantalising contract.

"The contract is tantalising," he observed, his green eyes twinkling, "for it is inevitable that the hearts will break badly, or you would not have given me the problem."

"I am saying nothing," I said.

"You do not have to, *mon cher ami*," he smiled. "Your honest face confirms that it is so. But I will win the first spade in dummy, praying that spades are not nine-nil."

"They are not, Poirot. East follows with the deuce."

"Suggesting a singleton," he nodded. "*Eh bien*, I play a diamond to my ace."

"West shows out," I told him. "Again, East contributes the deuce."

"*Regardez*, Hastings. In order to count the hand completely, an expert might cash his two club winners, expecting West to show out on the second round. Our expert would play another top trump and the ♡K. Then he would throw East in with a trump!"

"But Poirot!" I remonstrated. "That is the deliberate sacrifice of a trick."

"*Vraiment*. Yet the trick returns with interest. *Voila*! First, East, having only clubs, must concede a ruff and discard. Second, our expert South, having ruffed, plays out all his trumps to squeeze West in the majors. For I deduce that the defenders cards are *comme çi*." He sketched the full deal, and waited for me to signify my approval:

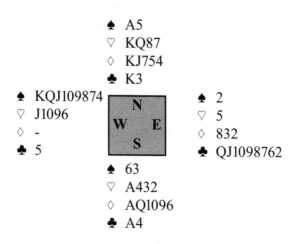

```
                    ♠  A5
                    ♡  KQ87
                    ◊  KJ754
                    ♣  K3
  ♠  KQJ109874   ┌─────────┐   ♠  2
  ♡  J1096       │    N    │   ♡  5
  ◊  -           │ W     E │   ◊  832
  ♣  5           │    S    │   ♣  QJ1098762
                 └─────────┘
                    ♠  63
                    ♡  A432
                    ◊  AQ1096
                    ♣  A4
```

"No, Hastings," he admonished, as I opened my mouth. "It is not yet the time to applaud. For I suspect that the good East is also an expert. To forestall the endplay, he would throw his ◊8 on the second round."

"Bravo, Poirot," I encouraged.

"*Oui, mon ami*, but unlike our run of the moulin expert, Hercule Poirot would foresee East's foresight. He would eliminate diamonds before tackling clubs. Now on leading the ♣K from the table, he would overtake with the ♣A. Then East can be thrown in with a small club to give declarer that ruff and discard, followed by that squeeze against West."

"But, Poirot …" I protested.

"No, Hastings, it is for me to protest. For by now, I understand the quality of the player in the East seat. *Sans doute*, he would contribute a high club on the first round, retaining the ♣2 to prevent the endplay."

"So your plan fails," I commiserated cheerfully.

"*Mais non, mon ami*. It has set the stage for my alternative strategy. While East distinguished himself by frustrating every attempt to throw him in, poor West has been stripped of his minor suits. When I play a second round of spades, he cannot refuse the trick, for it will give me a total of twelve. But when he captures he is between the *diable* and the deep blue *mer*, for a spade continuation will present me with a ruff and discard, while if he opens hearts, I will make all four tricks in that suit."

"*Magnifique!*" I exclaimed, forgetting myself.

Thank you, Hastings. After you chronicle the deal, as I am sure you will, some critic in the next century will no doubt call my dummy play *chapeau vieux*. But today, with contract bridge in its adolescence, I must confess I am pleased with myself. Now tell me about the murderer who played the hand. Who is he?"

"You have heard of Sir Piers Prendergast?"

"*Naturellement*. The richest man in London, and a fanatical card player. But surely not a murderer?"

"On the contrary. Last night he was poisoned in his Belgravia residence, while he was watching a rubber. The fatal dose was dropped into his port by one of the four players."

"How do you know that?" Poirot demanded.

"Except for Robinson, the ancient butler, who has been with the Prendergasts for nearly a century, nobody, apart from myself, had the opportunity."

"But you do not know which of the four players was guilty?"

"No."

"Yet you were there, *mon ami*. And the deed was committed under your very nose." He sighed theatrically. "Hastings, you had better tell me everything that happened."

I sighed in return. For, as my mind went back to my first meeting with Sir Piers, I knew that I had not covered myself with glory.

When Sir Piers Prendergast invited me to dine at his club, I had no idea why I was being so honoured. He was a reserved man of sixty with grey hair, poor eyesight and a diffident manner, and it was not until coffee and liqueurs were served that he came to the point of our meeting.

"I must admit, Captain Hastings, that I have been trying to secure the services of your friend, Poirot. But the man is impossible to reach. His housekeeper informs me that he is presently engaged in saving civilisation as we know it. I hoped you could intercede on my behalf."

"Sir Piers," I assured him, "as Hercule Poirot's right-hand man, I am so familiar with his methods that I am sure that I can assist you."

For some reason, the baronet seemed dubious, but he took a sheet of paper from his pocket. It contained the small slam, which later was to provide Poirot with such a challenge.

"That deal," he said, "was sent to me anonymously two days ago. It was accompanied by this typewritten letter.

"Dear Sir Piers, As a keen bridge player, you will undoubtedly find the enclosed hand fascinating. It may also interest you to know that the ingenious declarer is an equally ingenious multiple murderer, who will be attending your bridge party on Friday evening. I wish you luck in identifying the assassin and sincerely hope that you are not the next intended victim."

"I see that the letter is unsigned," I remarked.

"Anonymous letters usually are," he pointed out, somewhat condescendingly. "So what do you make of it, Hastings?"

"It could be a hoax," I said. "But for the moment it would be prudent to take it seriously. I shall be delighted to attend your soirée on Friday evening. Nobody will dare to raise a hand to you while I am present. Black tie, I presume?"

Sir Piers' house was the last word in luxury. One's feet sunk into the ancient Turkish silk carpets. One's eyes feasted with delight on the Cézannes and Renoirs which covered the walls. One's nose twitched with ecstasy at the bouquet of the venerable brandy in the antique balloon glass. One's mouth watered at the sight of the superb *canapés*. One's intellect responded sharply to the prospect of witnessing a feast of fascinating bridge.

And fascinating it was, for Sir Piers had gathered together four of the shining lights from the Mayfair Bridge Club, such fine players that he and I decided not to participate in order to watch them in action.

The four players cut for partners. Captain Maltravers, a dark man of thirty with a rakish expression on his handsome face, drew Lady Blythe. She was a beautiful, charming and wealthy widow who, since her husband had been mysteriously washed overboard while his yacht was moored in a tranquil Caribbean bay, seemed determined to enjoy every minute of her well-earned freedom and every penny of his enormous fortune.

Herr Müller was a bridge star from Austria, a country which was expected soon to rival America for world supremacy. He had no sense of humour, but a remarkably well-developed card sense. His partner was Gorik Hasek, a mystery man from middle Europe, whose impeccable manners and dashing good looks had taken London society by storm.

This was the first deal of the first rubber:

Love All. Dealer West.

Hasek
- ♠ AQJ2
- ♡ A86
- ◇ K97
- ♣ Q42

Lady Blythe
- ♠ K
- ♡ K9532
- ◇ Q432
- ♣ A103

Maltravers
- ♠ 87654
- ♡ Q1074
- ◇ -
- ♣ K987

Müller
- ♠ 1093
- ♡ J
- ◇ AJ10865
- ♣ J65

South	West	North	East
	1♡	Dble	3♡
4◇	Pass	5◇	All Pass

When Lady Blythe led the ♡3 and dummy appeared, Müller considered the situation without emotion. For twenty seconds he seemed more like a calculating machine than a man. Then he nodded sagely, called for dummy's ♡A and ruffed a heart. At trick three he advanced the ◊J and confidently ran it when Lady Blythe played low. With the spade finesse working, the rest was plain sailing.

"You read the hand beautifully, partner," Hasek congratulated him.

"Thank you," replied Müller, "but it was quite elementary. The opening lead told me that Lady Blythe had only one of the top hearts, for from KQxxx she would not have led a low card. With the ♣AK she would surely have led a club, so I placed her with the ace only. It followed that to have justified even the lightest opening bid she needed the ♠K and the ◊Q."

He gulped his brandy and held out his glass to be refilled by the ancient butler, Robinson. "Alternatively" he continued, "Lady Blythe could be very distributional, with a diamond void. My lead of the jack catered for both possibilities."

"You make it sound so easy," said Lady Blythe. "I wish I could analyse so lucidly."

"Oh, but you can, Lady Blythe," laughed Captain Maltravers. "It is one of your great strengths. Your naive manner deceived me when I first played against you, and I still have the scars to prove it. Now I recognise you for the tigress that you are – in the bridge sense, of course."

"Thank you, Captain Maltravers," she smiled. "I think," she added judiciously.

A few deals later, after both sides had scored substantially above the line, Lady Blythe had the opportunity to justify the Captain's high opinion of her cat-like powers and grabbed it with both claws.

I have rotated the hands for convenience.

East/West Game. Dealer East.

Maltravers
- ♠ 96
- ♡ 642
- ◇ AQ107
- ♣ 7542

Hasek   Müller

```
      N
   W     E
      S
```

Lady Blythe
- ♠ KQJ108754
- ♡ -
- ◇ 8653
- ♣ Q

South	West	North	East
			1♡
4♠	6♡	Pass	Pass
6♠	Dble	All Pass	

Lady Blythe's bidding may appear reckless. Having preempted on the first round, she might well have left further decisions to partner, but she probably reasoned that with two defensive tricks, Maltravers would have doubled, if only to warn her against sacrificing.

Hasek led the ♡K. Declarer ruffed and led the ♠K, Hasek discarding the ♡A. Müller took with the ♠A and played the ♣6. Lady Blythe, an emotional player, could not conceal her surprise when her ♣Q held the trick. She considered this windfall for a few moments, then smiled seraphically, drew trumps and led the ◇8. When Hasek played low, she let the eight run, and was soon claiming her improbable contract.

This was the complete deal:

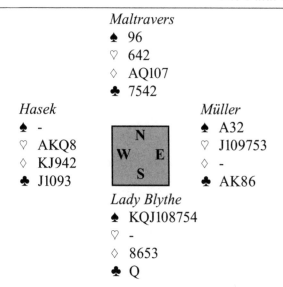

Maltravers
- ♠ 96
- ♡ 642
- ◊ AQ107
- ♣ 7542

Hasek
- ♠ -
- ♡ AKQ8
- ◊ KJ942
- ♣ J1093

Müller
- ♠ A32
- ♡ J109753
- ◊ -
- ♣ AK86

Lady Blythe
- ♠ KQJ108754
- ♡ -
- ◊ 8653
- ♣ Q

"What did I tell you, gentlemen?" asked Maltravers. "That my partner is a man-eater. And now she has proved it – in spades."

"Charming nonsense," responded Lady Blythe, "but nonsense nevertheless. When a fine player like Herr Müller underleads an ace, it does not require the instincts of a tigress to deduce his motive – even a poor little mouse could see that he hoped to find Mr Hasek with the ♣QJ or ♣Q10, and to collect a healthy penalty with two diamond ruffs."

"Exactly," agreed Müller. "The risk of finding the actual distribution was minimal. I am confident that my defence was correct."

"Ah!" said Maltravers. "So you find that playing well is more satisfying than playing successfully? How droll."

If looks could kill, Müller would have reduced the captain to a cinder. Calculating machine though he was, at that moment the Austrian looked every inch the cold-blooded killer.

But the gentlemanly Hasek came to the rescue. "My partner's defence deserved to succeed," he said. "The blame for our catastrophe was mine alone; when Lady Blythe played the ♠K, I should have thrown the ♣J, denying the queen."

Sir Piers was too good a host to permit any ill feeling to continue. He signalled to Robinson, his ancient butler, who mixed another pink gin for Lady Blythe, replenished the mens' brandy glasses, placed a decanter of port on the occasional table next to his master, and sat down in a state of total exhaustion.

After each side had sacrificed in turn to prevent their opponents from making a vulnerable game, Maltravers was given a chance to prove his mettle:

Game All. Dealer South.

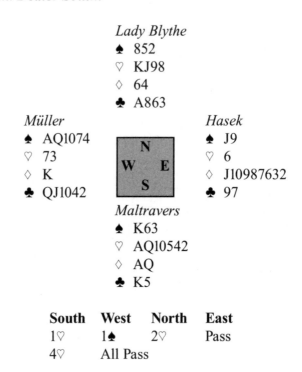

Lady Blythe
♠ 852
♡ KJ98
◇ 64
♣ A863

Müller
♠ AQ1074
♡ 73
◇ K
♣ QJ1042

Hasek
♠ J9
♡ 6
◇ J10987632
♣ 97

Maltravers
♠ K63
♡ AQ10542
◇ AQ
♣ K5

South	West	North	East
1♡	1♠	2♡	Pass
4♡	All Pass		

The captain won the club opening lead in hand and drew trumps, East showing out on the second round. He played the ♣A and ruffed a club, while Hasek discarded a diamond. Now he made the astonishing play of the ◇A from his hand. Even the phlegmatic Müller blinked before sheepishly contributing his king.

"Clever, very clever," said Sir Piers, who had been so absorbed in the bridge that his glass of port remained untouched.

"I concur," said the sporting Hasek. "Declarer's could place my partner with a singleton diamond. He had shown up with five clubs and two hearts as well as presumably five spades."

"But how did you know that the diamond king would drop?"

demanded the baronet.

"I think our friend the captain can explain his reasoning far better than I," said Hasek.

"There is no reason why it should," explained Maltravers. "But if Müller had followed with a small diamond, I had made my mind up to exit with the ♠K."

"What, and gift the defence three spade tricks?" I protested.

"Why not? After the three spade tricks, Müller would be forced to give me a ruff and discard," Maltravers explained.

"But tell me Captain," asked Lady Blythe, "what would have happened if the ◊K had not dropped and Mr Hasek had taken the second round of spades?"

"Then he could not have held a third spade to defeat me. I trust Müller's bidding unreservedly, and he would never make an enterprising overcall on as little as AQ10x, so the worst Hasek could do would be to cash one diamond. Then he too would be endplayed."

"So he would," agreed Lady Blythe, after taking a reflective sip of her pink gin, while the revitalised Robinson fussed around the guests.

"The play of either the diamond ace or the spade king both look wrong," said Sir Piers, "and I must confess I would never have thought of them. I would have contrived to lead spades from the table, hoping that East was asleep and would neglect to contribute his knave."

"And you might have succeeded had my pips not been proof against such an occurrence, Sir Piers," laughed Hasek, "for I often fall asleep at the bridge table when I have not played a contract all evening."

"Never mind," sympathised Lady Blythe. "Perhaps your luck will change in the new rubber."

It changed to the extent that the romantic Hasek drew the dazzling Lady Blythe as his partner, a prospect which gave him evident pleasure.

Love All. Dealer East.

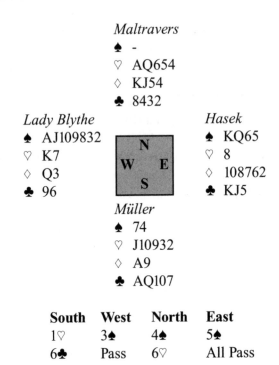

Maltravers
- ♠ -
- ♡ AQ654
- ◇ KJ54
- ♣ 8432

Lady Blythe
- ♠ AJ109832
- ♡ K7
- ◇ Q3
- ♣ 96

Hasek
- ♠ KQ65
- ♡ 8
- ◇ 108762
- ♣ KJ5

Müller
- ♠ 74
- ♡ J10932
- ◇ A9
- ♣ AQ107

South	West	North	East
1♡	3♠	4♠	5♠
6♣	Pass	6♡	All Pass

After a highly competitive auction, Müller found himself in a small slam, which, as the cards lay, should normally have been made with an overtrick. But Lady Blythe made the extraordinary lead of the ♠2!

I could sense the Austrian's thoughts as he studied this card. Obviously the lady was taking a risk to give her partner the lead. But why? It could only be because she wanted a club ruff. He paused to check his calculations, gave a little nod, ruffed the opening lead on the table and laid down the ace of hearts. When both defenders followed low, he nodded again, called for dummy's ♣8 and confidently ran it.

After Lady Blythe's ♣9 won the trick, she cashed the ♡K and gave the astonished declarer a sympathetic smile.

"I am lost in admiration, partner," smiled the gallant Hasek.

"It is Herr Müller who deserves your admiration," she demurred. "My defence could only have succeeded against an expert."

"This is true!" confirmed Müller, who was willing to take all the credit for her coup.

"Forgive me, Lady Blythe," interposed Sir Piers, "but would you be kind enough to explain your expert defence for the benefit of mere mortals like Hastings and myself?"

"Certainly," she replied, "though it was not as remarkable as you seem to think. The bidding marked Captain Maltravers with a spade void, so my lead could hardly cost. And if dummy held the ♡A, it might dissuade declarer from taking the winning trump finesse. Making the ♣9 was a bonus, but not a totally unexpected one."

"Very ingenious," said the baronet. "And you are right; the defence would never have worked against me. I should have taken every finesse, except that of the ♣8, and probably made thirteen tricks. Is that what you would have done, Hastings?"

"Probably," I admitted.

"So would I," agreed Captain Maltravers, with a derisive sneer, which suggested that his partner had been far too clever for his own good. The angry Austrian responded with a look that was truly homicidal.

On the next deal, Müller, in Two Spades, tranced for three minutes and proceeded to make nine tricks by means of a rare and complex squeeze.

"Well played, partner," sneered Maltravers. "That brilliantly conceived overtrick was worth waiting for. I am glad I managed to stay awake."

Müller, oblivious to sarcasm, nodded his acknowledgement of the barbed compliment, as he cut the cards in the direction of Lady Blythe.

As I watched her dealing, I was struck by her beautifully kept hands. They were the hands of a woman who never in her life held a duster or a dishcloth, but were they the hands of a murderess? She was about to prove that she had at least one of the qualities needed for that occupation – nerve!

East/West 60 Below. Dealer South.

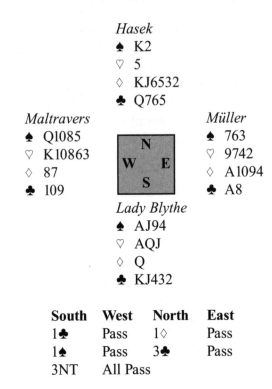

Hasek
♠ K2
♡ 5
◊ KJ6532
♣ Q765

Maltravers
♠ Q1085
♡ K10863
◊ 87
♣ 109

Müller
♠ 763
♡ 9742
◊ A1094
♣ A8

Lady Blythe
♠ AJ94
♡ AQJ
◊ Q
♣ KJ432

South	West	North	East
1♣	Pass	1◊	Pass
1♠	Pass	3♣	Pass
3NT	All Pass		

Maltravers led the ♡6 to his partner's ♡9 and declarer's ♡Q. Clearly, setting up the clubs would ensure eight tricks, provided they were no worse than 3-1. But, with the unfavourable spade lie, where would the ninth come from? If Lady Blythe had another diamond she could ignore clubs and set up diamonds, assuming a 3-2 break. While I was considering her options, she had made her decision: she pretended she did have a second diamond!

Crossing to the table with the ♠K, she led the ◊2. This was superbly reasoned. If Maltravers had the ace, he could do no harm; if Müller had it he would surely play low.

He had and he did. Declarer had her ninth trick and proceeded to establish clubs and claim.

"Too good for us," stated Maltravers. "That coup would have deceived many an opponent. So don't blame yourself, partner."

"I don't," said Müller stiffly. "It was correct to play low."

On reflection I thought Maltravers was being too kind and

Müller too complacent. It occurred to me that with a queen doubleton diamond, declarer might have started with the queen from hand, hoping for a 3-2 break and preserving dummy's ♠K as an entry to the long diamonds. But, as Poirot is fond of telling me, I am not a player of the first rank.

After Hasek had made an easy four hearts to win the rubber, our host suggested a short break, and he and I walked across to view his latest acquisition, a rather fetching ballerina by Degas.

"Whom do you suspect?" he demanded.

"I suspect everybody," I replied, in true Poirot fashion. "Even myself," I added, remembering one of Poirot's early cases.

"Then it is time to put our plan into effect," he said.

I nodded, took from my pocket the paper containing the deal which had been sent to Sir Piers, and strolled to the table where the players were sitting. I showed them only the North/South hands, but have repeated the whole deal here:

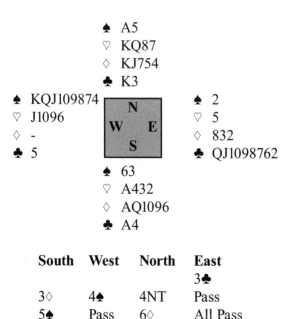

```
              ♠ A5
              ♡ KQ87
              ◇ KJ754
              ♣ K3
♠ KQJ109874              ♠ 2
♡ J1096         N        ♡ 5
◇ -          W     E     ◇ 832
♣ 5             S        ♣ QJ1098762
              ♠ 63
              ♡ A432
              ◇ AQ1096
              ♣ A4
```

South	West	North	East
			3♣
3◇	4♠	4NT	Pass
5♠	Pass	6◇	All Pass

"I was shown this hand recently," I said. "I was wondering what you experts would make of it."

As they studied the deal, Hasek was the first to speak.

"What a pity you omitted the defender's hands," he smiled

charmingly. "After seeing them I would undoubtedly find the perfect declarer play."

"I am afraid I never attempt abstract problems," said Lady Blythe. "To me, bridge is a game of psychology, instinct and flair. Without the vibrations one receives at the table, a hand holds no interest for me."

"My sentiments exactly," agreed Maltravers. "All I can say at this stage is that the contract appears to depend upon a throw in."

"That is obvious," said Müller. "And which one should be thrown in depends on how they play to the first two tricks."

I showed them the East/West hands and Müller, having the loudest voice, told us the solution, whereupon the four players dutifully went across to admire the Degas.

"What now?" whispered Sir Piers.

"I would swear that none of them had seen the deal before," I said. "It seems that your letter was a hoax."

"Isn't it possible that an ingenious murderer could also be an ingenious actor?" he suggested.

"True, Sir Piers. But remember that for many years I have been trained by Poirot to see through a masquerade. The deal was new to every one of them. I would stake my life on it."

Unfortunately it was Sir Piers who staked his life on it, and lost! A moment later, after sipping his port, he rose, gasped frantically for breath and fell heavily to the floor. I knelt beside him and searched for his pulse, but he was dead.

I telephoned for the police. Müller's suggestion that they played another rubber while we awaited their arrival was rejected, and he settled down to a game of solitaire, cursing the inconvenience.

Robinson, the ancient butler, was most distressed, but he carried out his duties like the loyal servant he was. As he gave me another brandy, he vowed to complain severely to the wine merchant about the quality of the port.

My old friend Superintendent Japp headed the investigation. The Baronet had been poisoned by a cyanide derivative, traces of which were found in his glass of port, but not in the decanter. Nobody had seen anybody tamper with the glass, but it was apparent that everybody in the room had the opportunity to do so. Not for the first time, Scotland Yard was completely baffled, and so, I must confess, was I.

"Hastings," said Poirot, when I had completed my narrative, "I congratulate you on your summary, for it was both revealing and concise. *Maintenant*, please be silent for a few minutes, while I exercise the little grey cells."

For five minutes he sat, as motionless as a statue, as if he was attempting to picture the events I had described. Then, suddenly, he leapt to his feet.

"*Milles tonnerres*!" he cried. "Of all the murders we have investigated, this is the most brilliant. I feel as if I should raise my hat to the perpetrators."

"Why the plural?" I demanded. "Do you mean that there was more than one?"

"*Mais oui*, Hastings. Let us begin with the anonymous letter. What was its purpose? To warn Sir Piers? Then why did the writer not name the murderer? Obviously he had another motive. But what?"

"I don't know, Poirot," I replied lamely.

"Think, Hastings. What was Sir Piers' reaction when he received the letter? First to contact me, Hercule Poirot, and when I refused to speak to him, to get in touch with you. And now that he is dead, what is my natural reaction? To forget my great task of saving civilisation as we know it, rush with you to the scene of the crime, interview the suspects, confer with *le bon* Superintendent Japp, and generally discommode myself to no purpose. Do you not see it, Hastings? They want to lure me from the security of my headquarters."

"But who are 'they', Poirot?"

"The Fatal Five, Hastings. Did I not tell you that in a few days I might actually accomplish their destruction?"

"So which of the bridge players killed Sir Piers?"

"None of them. It was Robinson, the ancient butler."

"But he has been with the family for nearly a century."

"That was the real Robinson, whose ancient body is probably at the bottom of the River Thames. The Robinson at your bridge party was that prince of impersonators, and executioner of the Fatal Five, the Liquidator."

"Was Sir Piers Prendergast a danger to the Five?" I asked.

"No, *mon Dieu*, but I am! And when I embark on the chase for the wild goose it is I who would be liquidated, Hastings. And none would suspect the killer, because he could appear as Japp, the Home Secretary or even you, Hastings. In fact ..."

He rushed towards me and ran his hands over my hair and face, searching for signs of a disguise. Finding none, he sank back into his chair.

"Forgive me, *mon ami*," he said. "One cannot be too careful."

Resisting the urge to retaliate by pulling Poirot's waxed moustache, I poured him a whisky and soda, and made a telephone call to Superintendent Japp. After a brief conversation I turned a red face towards the little Belgian.

"Poirot," I said. "An ancient body has been found floating on the Thames. The police have identified it as Robinson. He had been dead for two days."

"Then I was right."

"But Poirot. Do you realise what this means?"

"Of course. It means the murder was committed by the butler."

"Then how dare I publish the adventure? The murder must never be committed by a member of the lower orders. Our readers will never forgive me."

"But Hastings. He was the Liquidator, not the real butler."

"It makes no difference, Poirot." I told him, as I picked up my hat and walked to the door.

"Where are you going, *mon ami*?"

"To the Mayfair Bridge Club."

"And what do you expect to find there?"

"A better ending for my story," I said.

When I reached my car, which was parked a cricket pitch away from Poirot's front door, I was annoyed to discover that one of the tyres was flat. It took ten minutes to replace it with the spare and, when I arrived at the Mayfair Club, five minutes to make myself presentable enough to be admitted to the bridge room.

Hoping to find at least one of the players who attended Sir Piers' tragic party, I made for the small Duke of Cumberland room where the high stake table was located. To my surprise I found all four of them. Watching them play was an elderly lady who was introduced as the mother of Hasek, the charming mystery man from middle Europe.

"How nice it is to see you here," said Lady Blythe, as she sorted her cards.

"And a remarkable coincidence," said Maltravers, the saturnine and raffish captain. "It only needs that doddering old butler to turn up and we'll have all six witnesses to Prendergast's death."

"An appalling tragedy," observed Hasek.

"It was the greatest shock of my life," said Müller, who had dealt the hand. "Five Diamonds."

I took a seat between Maltravers and Lady Blythe, and this is what I saw:

Game All. Dealer East.

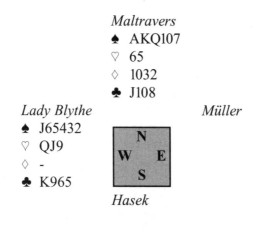

Maltravers
- ♠ AKQ107
- ♡ 65
- ◊ 1032
- ♣ J108

Lady Blythe
- ♠ J65432
- ♡ QJ9
- ◊ -
- ♣ K965

Müller

Hasek

South	West	North	East
			5◊
5♡	Pass	6♡	All Pass

On the assumption that Müller held eight diamonds, Maltravers did not expect Hasek to have more than one, but if he had two, West would not have a diamond to lead.

When Lady Blythe led the ♡Q and Maltravers tabled his dummy, Hasek thanked his partner warmly and exuded confidence from every pore. Müller threw the diamond ace. After assessing his prospects, Hasek won with the ♡A and continued with the ♡K, on which Lady Blythe followed smoothly with the ♡J! Whilst Hasek considered the implications of this remarkable stroke of fortune,

Lady Blythe let out an artful squeal of surprise as she contrived to find her ♡9, as though it had been concealed behind another card. But, Hasek, with an affectionate wink at his admiring mother, exited the ♡2!

Forced to win with her remaining trump, Lady Blythe had to choose her exit card. Müller's discards had been unhelpful; after the ◊A, he had followed with the ◊K and the ◊Q.

Clearly, declarer did not hold any spades, but what did he have in clubs? If he had the ace and queen, which seemed likely, a club exit would be fatal, since the jack would win the trick, and declarer's remaining losers would go on the winning spades. So Lady Blythe exited with a spade. Surely, declarer would not risk the Greek gift of the finesse, and would instead hope either to drop the ♠J in three rounds or, if necessary, fall back on the club finesse.

This was superbly reasoned, but Hasek *did* finesse, since the full hand was:

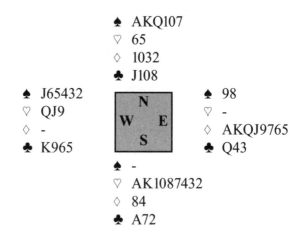

"Well done," said Müller generously. He seemed a different person from the unpleasant, humourless man I had observed during the previous evening.

"I am proud of you, Mishling," said Mrs Hasek, giving her son's hand a maternal squeeze.

"I assure you it was nothing," Hasek insisted. "I could see no hope for the contract, but clearly Lady Blythe could. If she was so desperate to avoid winning a trump trick, it had to be in my interests to force her to do so."

"My discards did nothing to help my partner," said Müller, offering an uncharacteristic apology. "It seems we are all far happier when we attempt to deceive. But soon," he added ominously, "our need for subterfuge will be at an end."

While they scored the rubber, the club's waiter appeared with a tray of drinks. To my surprise, it included a whiskey and soda for myself.

"We expected you to come," explained Maltravers, as the waiter left the room.

"You might almost say we willed you to arrive," added Müller.

"I never could stay away from an exciting game of bridge," I said somewhat nervously.

"Yes, we banked on that," smiled Hasek.

I was beginning to get an uncomfortable feeling that I had bitten off more than I could chew. Maltravers had left the card table and was standing menacingly in front of the door. I summed up the situation in a flash.

"You'll never get away with it," I warned them.

"Oh, I think we shall," replied Lady Blythe. "So far, our attempts to lure Hercule Poirot from his fortress have failed, but when he discovers his great friend is in our power, who knows what may happen?"

I looked around the room and did some rapid arithmetic. "There are five of you!" I exclaimed.

"The man is brighter than I thought," laughed Hasek. "He can actually count."

"Which could be a fatal weakness," said Müller.

"Perhaps I should reintroduce myself," said Hasek's mother. "When we last met I was the doddering old butler at Sir Piers party, busily poisoning his port."

"The Liquidator!" I cried triumphantly, for it seemed I had found a better ending to my story than I could ever have imagined. And a moment later, it got even better, for the door of the card room opened and the club's waiter burst in, not with a drinks tray, but with a Smith and Wesson revolver in each hand. He was followed by Superintendent Japp and several dozen armed detectives, who quickly handcuffed the Fatal Five. As they were dragged off to face justice, they vowed vengeance, and boasted that no prison could hold them.

I turned to the waiter. "I take it you're from Scotland Yard," I said.

"No, *mon ami*," he said. "You will have to guess again."

"Poirot!" I deduced, at the top of my form.

"I am sorry I had to arrange for your flat tyre, Hastings," he said, as he removed his wig, false nose and contact lenses. "I needed time to assume my disguise and get here before you."

"So you knew the Fatal Five would be here?"

"I was not certain, but I hoped my refusal to leave headquarters would make them desperate – and careless. I could not let you into the secret, Hastings, for only if you behaved naturally would my plan have worked."

"So you decided to make the supreme sacrifice?" I said.

"What do you mean, Hastings?"

"Your moustache."

"Ah, yes." He sighed mournfully, and stroked the upper lip which had once borne the luxuriant growth. "It will provide a moving finale for your story. It might even help your readers to overlook its fundamental flaw which no subsequent event can completely eradicate."

"What is that, Poirot?"

"The butler did it."

Killing Defence

If you come from a quaint, old-fashioned country, like Great Britain, I'll have more chance of convincing you that Christmas Day will fall on Good Friday than that a jury in an American murder trial could consist entirely of bridge players. In theory the odds against that happening are at least a billion to one, but our jury selection system can be exploited to turn it into an even-money bet. And if the process seems too fantastic for words, trust me. I'm a judge.

First, seventy-five candidates are auditioned. On average a dozen or so will have played the game, but because various low-life types don't make it to first base, the figure could be closer to twenty.

In the case of the People against Eleanor Blesco, the remaining non-players were weeded out during the ritual known as *voir dire*. Normally the lawyers assess prospective jurors for prejudice. But Jack Slattery was interested only in their ability to tell a ruff from a sluff. I admired his strategy. No sane jury would fall for his cockamanie defence, but twelve bridge players might.

If ever you decide to commit a murder, do it in America, where our trials are conducted to prevent our prisons from becoming overcrowded. For example, as presiding judge, I could reject anybody who seemed to have been influenced by the pre-trial publicity. This usually favours the defence. And the bridge buffs were so keen to get into the act that they lied through their teeth to prove that they were more neutral than the Swiss Red Cross. Another bonus was that was that the defence could reject ten candidates without showing cause, while the prosecution had to be content with six.

So Assistant District Attorney Manuel Delgado found himself up against seven women and five men, all drooling at the prospect of a week of sex, violence and bridge.

Manny Delgado was a tough-looking Hispanic with a fierce dark moustache, a face to match and a courtroom manner calculated to make the most hardened criminal quake in his boots. Yet he began his opening statement with the air of a man who had been handed a hot potato. His case was so strong that if he lost it he could look forward to a long spell of prosecuting first-offence jaywalkers. But public sympathy for a lady who had rid the bridge scene of a Partner from Hell was so intense that if she was convicted Delgado wouldn't win a popularity contest against the Boston Strangler.

And this lady was a defence attorney's dream. The man who observed that truth, goodness and beauty are but different faces of the same all, must have met Eleanor Blesco. Every man who met her wanted to take her to bed. Every woman wanted to take her shopping. I shall not desribe her effect on me, in case you think I wanted to find her not guilty.

The purpose of an opening statement is not to present an argument but to predict the evidence. Manny was dispassionate, fair and concise. Perhaps the potato was so hot that he wanted to drop it as quickly as possible into his opponent's lap.

These were the salient points of the prosecution's case:

1. After the final board of the Fairview Country Club's Open Pairs championship, Mrs Blesco had put an end to a bridge argument by hurling a heavy wooden board at her husband. It struck him between the eyes with such force that he fell to the floor, unconscious.

2. A fellow competitor, Doctor Mason, in an attempt to revive the patient, administered an injection of adrenaline.

3. Unknown to the doctor, Mr Blesco had an aneurism, a morbid dilation of an artery, and the injection predictably caused it to burst, with fatal consequences.

4. The aneurism had been detected a week earlier during a medical check up. Blesco had been informed, and would surely have told his wife, who was a qualified nurse.

5. Mrs Blesco knew that Doctor Mason would be present, and that he never went anywhere without his medical bag. She had previously seen him give an adrenaline injection to an elderly bridge player who had suffered a cardiac arrest after flooring a cast-iron vulnerable grand slam.

6. Relations between the Blescos had been deteriorating for some time. Several weeks before his death, Mr

Blesco hired a detective agency to follow his wife, whom he suspected of infidelity. The agency had found no direct evidence against her, but reported that on several occasions she managed to elude their detectives with such ingenuity that they were convinced they had been spotted.

7.   Mrs Blesco was her husband's main beneficiary, and his estate was worth more than $20 million.

Jack Slattery was a JFK lookalike, and one of the brightest young lawyers in the State. As he smiled at the jury it was love at first sight for all seven women and two of the men.

"May it please the court," he began. "Mr Delgado has outlined his case with commendable economy. I shall try to follow his example. I concede every point he made. Except one. When Eleanor Blesco tossed the board ..."

"Objection!" cried Delgado, leaping to his feet, "to the word tossed. We shall show evidence that the heavy wooden board was hurled with great force."

"Overruled," I said, coating the pill with several layers of Southern courtesy. "Perhaps we can save the semantics for later. And, Mr Delgado, as it's such a hot day you have the court's permission to object from a recumbent position."

"We will show," Slattery resumed, "that when Mrs Blesco caused the board to move in the direction of her husband, it was a gesture of extreme frustration, built up over six years of playing bridge with a man you will hear described as the most overbearing partner in the club, the county and the state."

As he prepared to sit down, he appeared to be struck by an afterthought, except that Jack didn't do afterthoughts. "Oh, one other thing. We'll be looking at a lot of bridge deals. Now I happen to love the game, but even my best friends will tell you I'm their favourite opponent. So if you're always two moves ahead of me in the analysis, please be patient."

The coroner's evidence was woefully lacking in entertainment value. The highlight was when he fulfilled Delgado's prediction by asserting that the board must have been propelled with considerable force, and Slattery declined to cross-examine. A cute fellow, Jack. When challenged, the expert witness is apt to get mighty stubborn. Having said that it was highly unlikely that a death was accidental, he delivers a body blow by changing 'unlikely' to 'impossible'.

The first witness to make the jury sit up and take notice was Annabella Cavanaugh, the bridge secretary of the Fairview Country Club. She was a well-stacked blonde, who was losing a costly battle to retain her looks, but seemed determined to go down fighting.

Having established her credentials, Delgado cut to the chase. "Miss Cavanaugh, in the club's Pairs Championship did you play the last three boards against the defendant?"

"Yes, and her poor husband." She shot a reproachful glance in Eleanor's direction. "Boards 31 to 33."

"Could you tell the court about the final board?"

"I was playing with a new member, Mr Hal Morgan."

Delgado smiled. "And you like to see that new members get good partners."

"Well, Mr Delgado, it's not for me to sing my own praises, but I play good Standard American and I've always got my bid."

"You certainly bid well on board 33."

The jurors turned dutifully to the deal in question in the folder provided by Slattery. Delgado considered the bridge testimony irrelevant, but he was too streetwise to incur the wrath of twelve angry bridge players by spoiling their fun.

East/West Game. Dealer South.

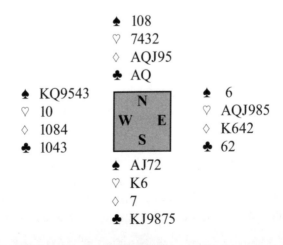

West	North	East	South
			1♣
Pass	1♦	1♡	1♠
Pass	2♡	Pass	3♣
Pass	4♣	Pass	5♣
All Pass			

"Mr Blesco led the ♡10," said Miss Cavanaugh. "Mrs Blesco won with the ace. Then, instead of giving her partner a ruff, she returned a spade."

She stared in turn at me, the jury, and the prosecutor, as if defying us to condone the preposterous switch.

"You thought this was odd?" asked Delgado.

"Most odd. After I'd followed to the first trick, Mr Blesco's ten had singleton written all over it."

"Did you make your contract?"

"No. I did the best I could, but as I had to pull trumps I couldn't stop Mr Blesco making two spade tricks. It was a very lucky defence, but that's bridge for you."

"Can you recall the reactions of the other players?"

"Well, Mr Morgan said 'bad luck, partner,' told me he hoped he'd see me in the bar and went out, probably to light a cigarette. We don't allow smoking in the bridge room."

"And Mr Blesco?"

"I was busy filling in the traveller, which should have been Mr Morgan's job, but I think Harry asked why she didn't give him his heart ruff. She said if he cared to look at her hand he'd see why, and he said he didn't need to look – he had a perfect memory, you know – and the next thing I knew she had picked up that heavy wooden board and thrown it at him with all her might."

She dabbed her eyes with a lace handkerchief.

"Miss Cavanaugh, I don't want to cause you distress, but where did the heavy wooden board land?"

"On Mr Blesco's lap. After it had hit him between the eyes." She broke off for some more dabbing. "Then he fell off his chair, and I called for Doctor Mason, who was siting two tables away. He gave Mr Blesco an injection, and a minute later poor Harry was dead."

"How did Mrs Blesco react?"

Miss Cavanaugh paused, as if to give her response due consideration. But she didn't fool anyone. She was moving in for the kill and milking every moment of it.

"She just sat there."

"Just sat there?" Delgado contrived to look shocked.

"Like she's sitting now. As cool as a cucumber."

We all studied Eleanor. The simile seemed apt. Delgado hammered home his advantage. "Didn't she weep? Shudder? Express regret?"

"No. As I said, she was as cool as a cucumber."

"Thank you," said Delgado, and left her, still dabbing.

When Slattery rose to cross-examine, he exuded compassion.

"Miss Cavanaugh, like Mr Delgado, I don't want to cause you distress, so let's talk about the play of board 33, rather than its tragic consequences."

"Very well," she agreed, with a brave little smile.

"You described the defence as very lucky. Would you mind if we looked at it from East's point of view?"

"Not at all," she said, welcoming a further chance to blacken the reputation of this particular East.

"Now, from the bidding, Mrs Blesco could tell that you had at least four spades and six clubs. And after your play to the first trick, she also knew you had two hearts and a singleton diamond."

"Why a singleton diamond? I might have been void."

"You're not doing yourself justice, Miss Cavanaugh. With a mere twelve count and a broken trump suit, you wouldn't contract for eleven tricks with a void in partner's suit, would you?"

"Well …" she began to hedge.

"Mind you," he grinned boyishly, "if I'd been in your seat, nobody who knew me would assume anything about my holding. But you've always got your bid, haven't you?"

"Well, I wouldn't say always."

"But you did. To the Assistant District Attorney. So having deduced your shape, Eleanor Blesco could count your likely tricks. Six clubs, one heart, and, with a correct view, two diamonds. So unless your spades were at least as good as ♠AQJx, you would go one down after a spade return. Do you agree with these calculations?"

"What calculations? It was nothing more than a lucky guess. Any real bridge player would have returned a heart."

"They might," concurred Slattery, "if they were sitting opposite an expert partner. An expert would not have ruffed the second round of hearts and the contract would still have gone down. However, in view of Mr Blesco's criticism of his wife's play, he didn't seem like an expert on board 33."

"I'm afraid I must disagree," she almost snapped.

By this time the jury had decided that Anabella Cavanaugh was not their favourite person. Two of them – life masters – shook their heads at her deeply flawed analysis, and the other ten soon followed suit.

"OK," Slattery smiled. "Suppose she had given Mr Blesco the heart ruff he was begging for. Once his trumps had been reduced to two, declarer could set up the diamond suit for three spade discards. You would have found that line, wouldn't you?"

"Of course. I know how to take a ruffing finesse. But I still say it was a lucky defence."

"You don't concede that Mrs Blesco could have read a hand that well?"

"Frankly, I don't."

"You don't like her very much, do you?"

Suddenly there was silence in court. Before poor Anabella could repair the damage, Slattery gave her the old one-two.

"Let me put it another way. You liked Mr Blesco a lot, didn't you?"

"I'd known him a long time."

"And before he married, he was your regular partner?"

"I played with him fairly often."

"Two or three times a week?"

"Sometimes."

"And you often went away with him, didn't you? To play in the national tournaments."

"Yes."

"Often for a week or more?"

"I don't care for your insinuations, Mr Slattery."

Delgado was already on his feet. "Nor do I, your honour. The witness is not on trial."

"Quite right, Mr Delgado," I ruled, suppressing my disapproval of the cliché. "Mr Slattery, I don't know where you're going with this." I know a judge is supposed to be a man of few words and many sentences, but I decided to give the voters another dose cracker-barrel humour. "But it isn't a federal offence for an unmarried couple to go away for a week of bridge, even if it means crossing the state border."

"My apologies to your honour and to you, Miss Cavanaugh. The only thing I was implying was that it must have been a blow when Mr Blesco dropped you for another partner."

"He didn't drop me," she snapped. "We stopped playing together by mutual agreement."

"I see. Who first suggested it?"

"I beg your pardon?"

"Well, unless the two of you chanted 'Let's dissolve the partnership' in unison, one of you must have suggested it. Was it Mr Blesco?"

"It may have been. I don't remember."

"Really?" He studied his notes. "You told us you were filling in the traveller while the Blescos discussed board 33."

"I wouldn't call it a discussion. Harry and I used to have some very rewarding discussions, but she hardly opened her mouth."

He nodded thoughtfully, to give the jury time to contrast Anabella's spiteful mien with the sad expression on Eleanor's lovely vulnerable face.

"Now according to your testimony, you did not see Mrs Blesco throw the board?"

"I said no such thing!"

"You stated that you were filling in the traveller and the next thing you knew she had picked up that heavy wooden board and thrown it at him with all her might."

"Yes," she agreed warily.

"You used the words 'she had'. The pluperfect tense. It denotes action completed before some moment in time, specified or implied."

"That's too deep for me, Mr Slattery."

"And for me, Miss Cavanaugh, but I have the advantage of quoting from the dictionary. If you had seen what happened, surely you would have said 'she picked up' and 'threw' that heavy wooden board you're so fond of describing."

"Objection!" roared Delgado. "He's badgering the witness."

"I don't think so, Mr Delgado," I mediated. "He was being sarcastic and I find it hard to visualise a sarcastic badger. However, Mr Slattery, it might be a good idea to save your titbits for your grand finale."

"Thank you, your honour," he said. "I was about to say that I have no further questions, unless Mr Delgado surprises us by producing an eye witness."

The most interesting of the other prosecution witnesses was the head of the enquiry agency Blesco had hired to investigate Eleanor. He related how she once made a sudden turn into a busy department store. When his detective followed a few seconds later, she had vanished into the crowd. He described three other instances of her uncanny ability to elude highly trained operatives. On each occasion she had arrived home several hours later. Slattery had a ball. By the end of his cross-examination, the witness admitted that what he had categorised as Eleanor's evasive actions were simply part of the erratic behaviour patterns of any American woman on a shopping spree.

Delgado was trying not to look grim, but he knew that after Miss Cavanaugh's sorry performance, the momentum had passed to the defence. Once doubt had been cast on the contention that Eleanor had hurled the bidding with intent to kill or injure, the rest of the evidence began to look depressingly unsubstantial.

To use the pluperfect tense, the prosecution had had a bad day.

Batting first for the defence was Will Shaw, the club chairman. Will was a handsome, grey-haired man, who had made a fortune in the used car business, probably because he looked more like a judge than I did. Fortunately, he had no political ambitions.

Love All. Dealer South.

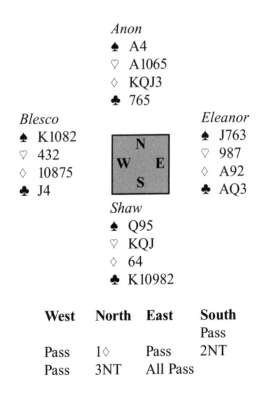

Anon
- ♠ A4
- ♡ A1065
- ◇ KQJ3
- ♣ 765

Blesco
- ♠ K1082
- ♡ 432
- ◇ 10875
- ♣ J4

Eleanor
- ♠ J763
- ♡ 987
- ◇ A92
- ♣ AQ3

Shaw
- ♠ Q95
- ♡ KQJ
- ◇ 64
- ♣ K10982

West	North	East	South
			Pass
Pass	1◇	Pass	2NT
Pass	3NT	All Pass	

"Yes, I recall the deal," he told Slattery as we all studied board 8. "Harry Blesco began with the ♠2, which ran to my queen. I played a diamond to the king. Eleanor won and cleared spades. I cashed four rounds of hearts and called for a club from dummy."

"Could I ask you to slow down a little, Mr Shaw?" requested Slattery. "The jury has probably kept up with you, but I haven't." He frowned at his copy of the deal. "Thanks. I'm with you now. You played a small club, presumably trying to steal your ninth trick ..."

"Yes, and the ♣Q appeared on my right. I assumed Eleanor had split her honours and Harry Blesco had bared his ace." He noticed a few blank faces amongst the jury. "Oh, I forgot to mention that he'd pitched a small club on the fourth heart, while his wife threw a spade. By now I'd been kidded into believing I had a count of the hand – it looked like Harry had the diamonds guarded, so he was forced down to a singleton club. So I played low, and when Blesco produced the ♣J, I knew I'd been hornswoggled."

"Bad luck, Mr Shaw."

"Great defence, Mr Slattery. If Eleanor had played her ♣A, I had nine on top. After a low club, my only realistic option would be to go up with the king and hope. That ♣Q was a gem. No other word for it."

"And what was Mr Blesco's word for it?"

"He asked her why the hell she hadn't ducked the first round of diamonds. You can see that wouldn't have made a scrap of difference. But he had to pick on something."

"Not one word of praise?"

"None. Why should he break the habit of a lifetime? If Eleanor had saved him from drowning by yanking him out of the sea, he'd have bawled her out for messing his collar."

At this point Delgado blew a gasket. I instructed the jury to disregard every word from 'why should he' to 'collar'. The spectacle of twelve jurors attempting to erase thirty odd words from their memory banks is a sight to behold.

Meanwhile, Manny was ranting on. "In fact I deplore this entire line of questioning. I am willing to concede that the defendant is a fine player whose husband didn't appreciate her. But if this court should send out the message that Mr Blesco had it coming, we're going to see a lot of merry widows at the bridge table."

"Well, Mr Delgado," I chided him gently, "since your objection has the distinct flavour of a closing speech, I think we'll let Mr Slattery respond to it."

"Your honour," said Jack, "our entire defence hinges on Eleanor Blesco's state of mind when she picked up board 33. Every factor contributing to her emotions at that fateful moment may be vital."

"Very well. You may proceed."

"Mr Shaw," he proceeded, "your tournament contained an astonishing proportion of challenging deals."

"It certainly astonished me. My wife, who directed the event, also organised the pre-dealt hands. When I accused her of salting the mine, she took the fifth," he added with a chuckle.

"Well congratulate her on board 9, which you also played against the Blescos." After the inevitable rustling, we found ourselves gazing at the following.

East/West Game. Dealer West.

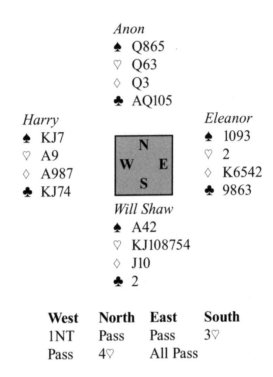

Anon
- ♠ Q865
- ♡ Q63
- ◇ Q3
- ♣ AQ105

Harry
- ♠ KJ7
- ♡ A9
- ◇ A987
- ♣ KJ74

Eleanor
- ♠ 1093
- ♡ 2
- ◇ K6542
- ♣ 9863

Will Shaw
- ♠ A42
- ♡ KJ108754
- ◇ J10
- ♣ 2

West	North	East	South
1NT	Pass	Pass	3♡
Pass	4♡	All Pass	

"Harry thought about his opening lead," said Shaw. "Finally he decided the ace of trumps was the least of four evils. Then he switched to the ◇A, and Eleanor encouraged with the six. A second diamond went to her king."

"Mr Shaw," Slattery interrupted, "before you tell us what she did then, could you describe the thought processes of an expert in the East seat?"

"Objection!"

"Yes, Mr Delgado?" I sighed wearily.

"We have no evidence that Mr Shaw is an expert witness."

"Then let's allow him to respond and we'll find out."

When Manny had subsided, Will Shaw continued: "In view of Harry's no trump opening, she would know that I was short on points and long on trumps. I probably had six tricks in hearts, one in spades and an unknown number in clubs. There is an inference that I have the ♠A, because if West held that card he might well have cashed it before playing a second diamond."

He hesitated in order to assess how many jurors were up to speed. After half of them nodded, he proceeded. "I believe that most experts would envisage the actual layout and do what Eleanor did."

"And what was that?"

"She switched to a small club."

"Round to dummy's ♣AQ10?" asked Slattery in awed tones.

"Looks like suicide, doesn't it? But it's the only card to break up the squeeze against West."

He went on to explain the four-card ending which would have cooked Harry's goose.

"Thank you, Mr Shaw," said Slattery. "Once again I'd like you to tell us how Mr Blesco greeted the expert play."

"When Eleanor returned that club he let out a groan of disbelief. Sounds hammy, but that was routine for Harry. Then when the board was over he gave her both barrels. He'd never seen such a crackpot defence. Had she never heard about leading through strength and up to weakness?"

"Didn't she explain about breaking up the squeeze?"

"No. It would have shown him up for what he was, and she's too much of a lady to do a thing like that."

"Was Mr Blesco always so quick to blame and slow to praise?"

"No. He would never have been voted partner of the year, but he always played with women and if they were cute enough to confine their comments to 'thank you, Harry' and 'I'll remember that, Harry', then he could be quite human." He reflected for a while. "At first, Eleanor fitted the bill."

"What changed?"

"When they married, he was the better player by a street. Aggressive bidder, smart declarer. He used to put the fear of God into weak opponents, and to be fair, at times he could put the best of us under pressure. He taught her a lot, no doubt about that. Then she began to study the game. And I mean study. I lent her her first dozen books. Within two years she could have written them. Today I doubt if there's a better defender in the state. With a partner of her own standard she could go right to the top."

"Do you think he realised that?"

"He suspected it. That's why he made sure that she never got the chance to find out. And we know what he did when she produced something magical. Talked and talked until it turned back into a pumpkin."

Promising metaphor, but needed a little polish, I thought, as Delgado began to cross-examine.

"Mr Shaw, will you agree that Harry Blesco was an overbearing, intolerant bridge player who goaded his wife without mercy?"

Shaw was amazed. "Yes, I would," he said.

"So would I," said Delgado, and sat back triumphantly.

Will Shaw was replaced by the defence's second witness, Millicent Summerville. She was a widow of ninety-six, but described her age as 'nearly a hundred'. She didn't mind her partners playing Standard American, as long as they let her play Culbertson. After half a century of landing in contracts ranging from unsound to impossible she had become a redoubtable card player.

"Mrs Summerville," asked Slattery, "how long have you been a member of the Fairview Country Club?"

"Seventy years come Saturday fortnight. They've fixed up a surprise party I'm not supposed to know about."

"I'm sure you'll enjoy it."

"I shall, as long as the champagne is French." She stared ominously at the jury. "And as long as nothing prevents Eleanor Blesco from attending."

This was too much for Manny. Only the Mafia were allowed to threaten juries. "Your honour!" he protested. "Would you ask Mr Slattery to control his witness?"

Nothing could improve the chilling stare she gave him. Except, perhaps, a lorgnette.

"Who is this man?" she demanded.

"He is Mr Delgado," I explained patiently. "He's an Assistant District Attorney."

She gave Manny a nod of understanding. "A word of advice, young man. Be polite to your elders and betters or you'll remain an assistant for the rest of your life."

Trying to control cantankerous nonagenarians is a no-win strategy. I signalled to Jack Slattery, who came gallantly to the rescue.

"Mrs Summerville, may I refer to board 14 in your folder? You played against the Blescos. I understand you and your partner were East/West."

"Yes. They keep offering me a privileged spot in an invalid chair facing north, but I like to move about while I still can. Remember that when you're my age."

She examined the diagram. "I see you've rotated the deal for convenience. That's very thoughtful of you. You may call me Millicent."

Love All. Dealer South.

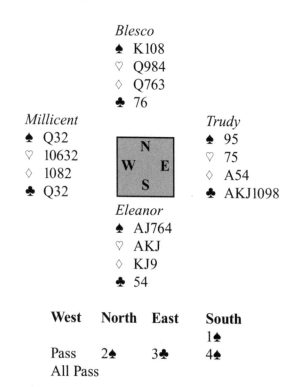

Blesco
- ♠ K108
- ♡ Q984
- ◊ Q763
- ♣ 76

Millicent
- ♠ Q32
- ♡ 10632
- ◊ 1082
- ♣ Q32

Trudy
- ♠ 95
- ♡ 75
- ◊ A54
- ♣ AKJ1098

Eleanor
- ♠ AJ764
- ♡ AKJ
- ◊ KJ9
- ♣ 54

West	North	East	South
			1♠
Pass	2♠	3♣	4♠
All Pass			

"Do you want me to talk you through the play?" she enquired, after examining the deal briefly.

"Yes please, Millicent."

"I led the ♣2. My partner, Trudy Rosenblum, cashed two rounds before switching to a heart. Eleanor won and quickly led the ♠J. Just as quickly, I covered with my queen." She grinned wickedly at the jury. "I expect you're thinking the old lady is one of those patsies who always covers an honour with an honour. Yes, you are – I can tell from your faces. Well, Eleanor is enough of an expert to know a fellow expert when she sees one. If a strong West covers, she must have something to protect. And this could only be ♠Q9xx. Tell me when you've absorbed that nugget and I'll continue."

"I think we're ready, Mrs Summerville," I intervened. "We've all spent a sleepless night boning up on our card play."

"Good for you, judge. And the name is Millicent. Eleanor played a diamond to her king and now played a second spade to dummy's eight. Unsuccessfully as you will see," she added with satisfaction.

"And then?"

"Eleanor said 'Well played, Millicent'. I said, 'Well played, Eleanor'."

"And Harry Blesco?"

She pondered. "I'm wondering how to put this."

"It's alright, Millicent," I advised her. "In a murder trial, it is not necessarily unsporting to speak ill of the dead."

"Oh, that wasn't what was worrying me. I was wondering how to do justice to his appalling antics. He looked like a warthog with toothache. And poor Eleanor sat waiting patiently for the outburst. He started pooping, as warthogs do, and suddenly I had enough. I said, 'Harry, you don't know what your talking about.' For a moment I thought he was going to hit me, but as usual his saint of a wife came to the rescue. She got as far as 'If you take a look at the hands, Harry,' but he just shouted her down."

"Can you tell us his exact words?"

"No. I only remember one word, and it was unprintable."

It was time for some more diplomacy. "Mr Slattery, I think we should respect the wishes of a lady who remembers the days when we spoke the language of Nathaniel Hawthorne and Louisa M Alcott."

"Agreed, your honour," said Slattery. "Millicent, what happened after Mr Blesco's outburst?"

"Didn't you know? Eleanor threw the board at him?" After she detonated this bombshell, I let the hubbub almost run its course before using my gavel. This gave Jack Slattery time to recover. It was clearly a shock to him, which greatly surprised me.

"We are talking about board Fourteen?" he asked weakly. "Not board Thirty-Three?"

"Of course."

"Did it hit him?"

"Not exactly. It skedaddled across the table and onto his lap. He picked it up, looked daggers at her, and tossed it back. It came to rest somewhere in no-man's land."

"Had she ever thrown a board before?"

"Thrown, tossed, pushed? Yes."

"When constructive discussion had become impossible?"

"They were always impossible. If she'd been given a chance to explain why she played me for queen-nine to four trumps, the loss of face would be more than he could bear. When she threw the board she was really throwing him a lifeline."

Slattery thanked her, sat down and passed the hot potato to Manny.

"Millicent," he began.

"You may call me Miss Summerville."

"When the defendant threw the board, you say it skidded across the table and into his lap?"

"Not skidded, skedaddled. I'm sorry to say the word seems to have gone out of fashion, like courtesy."

"Whatever word we use, Eleanor Blesco's action was a violent one, wasn't it?"

"Many years ago, when I won the state table tennis championship, we would have called her wrist action a backhand flick. Not the most violent of shots, but a ping-pong ball isn't a violent object."

"But a heavy wooden board is."

"Didn't you know, Mr Delgado? This particular board was made of soft brown plastic. A housefly would have found it violent, but not a big strong man like Harry Blesco."

"Surely ..."

"Please let me finish. We were in the final of the Open Pairs. The consolation event was taking place in another room. They were using the other set of plastic boards, all thirty-two of them. So, as we were using an eleven-table Howell movement, we had to make do with a wooden one for board 33. You really should speak sharply to your investigating officers for overlooking an important fact like that."

It was not Manny's finest hour. As Millicent left the witness box, she winked at the jury, as if to remind them that Eleanor was expected at her party, or else. The Mafia had nothing on Millicent.

When Eleanor took the stand, the wave of sympathy from the body of the court was almost tidal. She wore a severe black two-piece which was designed to minimise her elegant curves, but failed. In the words of Eugene O'Neill, mourning became her. As she took the oath in a soft mezzo soprano voice, I could find only one word to do justice to her delicate beauty. Garbo.

I hastily pulled myself together. I had an office to fulfil, an impartial trial to run, and a defendant to acquit.

Slattery's first question was an attention getter, to say the least.

"Mrs Blesco, did you hate your husband?"

"No," she replied. "I have never hated anyone."

Amazingly, we believed her.

"Did you love him?"

"I did once. He could have been a fine man."

"Not according to some of his bridge acquaintances."

"Bridge is like that. It brings out the best in some, and the worst in others. Harry was one of the others, I'm afraid."

"Why do you think that was?"

"He played by instinct. Slow play irritated him. He had the intellect to analyse a hand deeply, but not the temperament."

"And you?"

"I'm not like Harry. My instincts aren't very sharp. But I love to think through a problem."

"Yet Harry Blesco was a business consultant and a very successful one."

"I know. When he talked about his client's problems I realised how easy it is to give advice when you're not emotionally involved. All you have to do is help them make a few simple choices. Expand or retrench. Diversify or rationalise. I've learned all the jargon, you see. Consultants are like computers – they think binary."

"Don't bridge players? To finesse or play for the drop?"

"Sometimes, Mr Slattery. At other times you must think laterally. Every opponent is different. Every hand is a minefield."

"We've seen some examples of the way you think, Mrs Blesco. Would you care to give us another?"

"You know very well I would," she smiled. "It's on the last page of your folder."

As we turned eagerly to the deal, I knew exactly what Slattery was up to. He wasn't showing off Eleanor's bridge, he was showing off Eleanor. The messenger is the message. He could have asked her for the recipe for French onion soup and the effect would have been the same. Everything she did or said would bear the stamp of a woman to whom revenge was unthinkable, violence repugnant and murder impossible. I glanced at the last page, half expecting it to begin with the words 'First peel your onions.'

North/South Game. Dealer North.

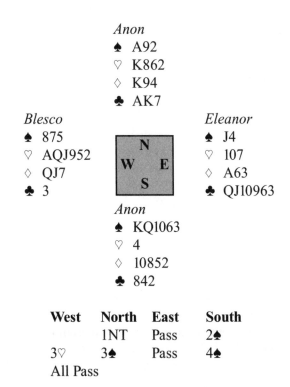

```
                    Anon
                    ♠ A92
                    ♡ K862
                    ◇ K94
                    ♣ AK7
Blesco                              Eleanor
♠ 875              N                 ♠ J4
♡ AQJ952       W       E            ♡ 107
◇ QJ7                               ◇ A63
♣ 3               S                 ♣ QJ10963
                    Anon
                    ♠ KQ1063
                    ♡ 4
                    ◇ 10852
                    ♣ 842
```

West	North	East	South
	1NT	Pass	2♠
3♡	3♠	Pass	4♠
All Pass			

"I tried to discuss this deal with Harry the night before he died," said Eleanor, without emotion. "We had played it that evening in a match. Harry couldn't understand why I defended as I did. He believed it was either instinct or luck. I prayed that this time I could actually get through to him."

"And did you?"

"I tried, I really tried. Harry had led his singleton club. Declarer won, drew trumps and led a heart towards the king. Harry rose and played a second round to dummy's king. Declarer pitched a club. Then she ruffed a heart and led the ◊10 towards the table. Harry covered with the knave, dummy played the king, and I ducked."

"On general principles?"

"Not entirely." She waited until we had all finished studying the hand and had turned our faces toward her, suitably expectant.

"By now," she explained, "I knew Harry's exact heart holding and it was clear that he had nothing in the black suits. In theory he would need both outstanding diamond honours to justify a vulnerable overcall at the three level. But Harry always played the players. Declarer was a very sweet lady who thought doubling opponents into game was the eighth deadly sin. Her partner was the opposite. She loved to punish the opposition, but on a previous board she'd doubled Harry and missed a vulnerable game for a 200 penalty."

"Not a profitable trade."

"No. So Harry may have been light for his bid. Should I play him for the queen of diamonds? He was the type of player who might play the jack from queen-jack or jack-ten. Then I realised it didn't matter. I could afford to duck the first round anyway. I had a complete count of the hand. Declarer needed two diamond tricks for her contract. If she had the queen, it was on ice, so I had to play on the assumption that Harry had split his honours and stop her from establishing her fourth diamond. It all depended on timing."

"So what happened when you ducked the trick?"

"Harry won the second round and played a heart, forcing declarer's last trump. Then, when diamonds were cleared I was able to lock declarer in dummy with a third club. Her long diamond was waste paper."

"Very satisfying," commended Slattery. "But wouldn't an instinctive player have ducked, just as you did?"

"Possibly. Harry evidently thought so."

"What did he say when you explained your thought processes?"

"He didn't believe me. And that made me feel sad, because he should have known that I hate lying."

"What about the time when you made him happy by saying

'yes, Harry' and 'I'll remember that next time, Harry'?"

"I was a very poor player. As I became more competent, I cultivated the useful art of saying nothing. And every now and again I'd try to get him to look at my hand and work things out for himself. But I think he was afraid to do that."

"Did you mean to kill him when you threw what the prosecutor and his witness unanimously and frequently describe as 'the heavy wooden board'?"

"No."

"Did you mean to hurt him?"

"No."

"Then why did you throw it so hard?"

"Because I thought it was a light plastic board."

Slattery decided to take a chance. It was bad form for a defence attorney to cross-examine the defendant, but with Delgado waiting in the wings it might be good tactics to forestall him.

"Mrs Blesco," he almost scoffed, "do you really expect the jury to believe that?"

"I wouldn't blame them if they didn't. I know it was an accident, but I shall never forgive myself for causing his death."

"Then please explain your mistake."

"After the last board but one, I wanted some coffee, so I went to the machine outside the room and got myself a cup. When I returned, the other players were sorting their cards and mine were on the table in front of me. I know it wasn't the thing to do, but Harry always does it. By now you must have gathered that he was a control freak."

"I think we got the message," Slattery agreed gravely. "And where was the heavy wooden board?"

"At the time it must have been on the low table beside Harry. He always liked the card table cleared for action. When the hand was over and the argument began, I hadn't noticed the board. I picked it up, just as I had a hundred times before, willing him to look at my hand and tell me I'd played it well."

"And then?"

"I threw it towards him out of sheer frustration. You know the rest."

"We know what the club secretary, Miss Cavanaugh said. She claimed that Harry's comments were constructive. And that your response was unspeakably violent."

"I know, and I don't blame her for saying that."

"Do you think she would verify your story about going off for coffee?"

"I don't know. Fortunately, her partner, Mr Hal Morgan would. So could two people I met at the coffee machine."

I didn't doubt the truth of this, but it made me feel uneasy. Why hadn't Slattery called these witnesses? It could only be because Eleanor's testimony was news to him. And he was a conscientious attorney.

"But have you any witnesses who saw you throw the board?" he enquired hopefully.

"I have one."

"Who?"

"Myself."

Slattery had no answer to that. "Thank you, Mrs Blesco. I have no further questions."

Delgado rose. It was his last shot and he desperately needed to make it tell.

"According to the medical evidence, the board struck your husband with considerable force. Are you seriously asking us to believe that throwing it was a gesture of frustration?"

"I'm not asking you to believe anything. I am simply telling you the truth, as I swore to do."

"And are you asking us to believe that when you picked up the board you failed to notice that it wasn't one of the plastic ones you usually throw at him?"

"Not until it left my hand. My only thought was to get him to look at my cards and see for himself why I had to break up that squeeze."

"It was a tragic coincidence that your husband was suffering from an aneurism, wasn't it?"

"Yes, it was."

"But you knew nothing about it?"

"Not until I saw the results of the autopsy."

"But surely Harry Blesco must have mentioned it?"

"I would have thought so. Yet he didn't."

"I put it to you that he must have done."

"No, Mr Delgado. I wish he had, I really wish he had."